THE TRIAL OF JESUS

THE TRIAL OF JESUS

VAL GRIEVE

OM Publishing
Bromley, Kent.

First published 1990
Reprinted 1991

Quotations from the Bible, unless otherwise stated, are from the
New International Version, © 1978 by the New York International
Bible Society, published in Great Britain by Hodder & Stoughton Ltd.

British Library Cataloguing in Publication Data

Grieve, Val
The trial of Jesus.
1. Jesus Christ. Trial
I. Title
232.9'62

ISBN 1–85078–066–8

OM Publishing is an imprint of Send The Light
(Operation Mobilisation)
PO Box 48, Bromley, Kent, England, BR1 3JH

Production and Printing in England by
Nuprint Ltd, Station Road, Harpenden, Herts, AL5 4SE.

Contents

Dedication

Dedicated to the Manchester City Mission (of which I am Chairman) and, also, my friend who got arrested!

Introduction

I shall never forget one of my first visits to court as a young law student. The man in the dock was on trial for murder. At that time the death sentence was still in force. There was an electric atmosphere in court, which is no longer present now that the death penalty has been abolished. As Dr Samuel Johnson has remarked, 'When a man knows he is to be hanged in a fortnight, it concentrates his mind wonderfully.' This was true not only of the accused but of all of us in court that day. Facing the accused was his judge, austere in wig and gown. On one side was Counsel for the Prosecution; on the other Counsel for the Defence. The jury sat, like a small and increasingly uneasy audience, at the side of the court. I remember watching the accused man's anxious face as the trial came to an end. The jury went out. The jury came back. Their verdict was 'Guilty'.

There then followed the grim procedure of passing the death sentence. In accordance with custom the judge placed a black cap on his head over his wig and then declared to the prisoner:

The jury have found you guilty of murder. The sentence of the court is that you be taken from this place to a lawful prison and thence to a place of execution and there suffer death by hanging and that your body be buried in the precincts of the prison in which you have last been confined before your execution. And may the Lord have mercy on your soul.

Then the chaplain standing by the judge added, 'Amen.'

Many years have gone by since that day. As a lawyer I have watched or followed many trials. Somehow they have a fascination all of their own. When one judge retired recently he claimed that courts offer the world's best free entertainment. John Mortimer (the author of the famous 'Rumpole' stories) has even suggested in his introduction to the book *Famous Trials* that one of our British contributions to world civilisation is the achievement of having produced most of the best murder trials in the long history of crime!

What is the most significant trial that has ever taken place? Is it that of the Greek philosopher, Socrates? The indictment of the city of Athens against him was, 'Socrates does evil. He does not believe in the gods whom the city believes in, but introduces other new deities. He corrupts the youths. Punishment—death.' History records that, when at the end of his hasty trial he was condemned to death, he showed no resentment. He said to his jurors, 'The hour of departure has come, and we go our ways. I to die and you to live. Which is better, God only knows.' He then drank the fatal cup of hemlock

8

which was given to him. So died Socrates, nobly and unafraid.

Or is the most significant trial that of the French heroine Joan of Arc? At a time when England and Burgundy were fighting against the French, Joan, a peasant girl aged thirteen, believed that God spoke to her telling her to save France. She failed to persuade the French Commander that this was the case but in February 1429 she went on to prophesy that the French would be defeated near Orleans. As a result she was granted an audience with the Dauphin of France. He appeared in disguise and was astonished when Joan recognised him. She was then granted permission to lead the French army against the British. Wearing white armour and carrying a banner inscribed 'Jesus, Maria' she led the French forces and routed the English. But subsequently the armies of Burgundy captured Joan and sold her to the English. She then appeared before a formidable Ecclesiastical Tribunal of twenty-two theologians and eleven lawyers. She was accused of witchcraft and heresy. Though only nineteen she defended herself with great skill. 'I do indeed believe in the Church here below. But I fall back on God. I submit to him; I rest upon him.' Despite her plea she was burned to death in 1431. As the flames rose around her she was heard to cry, 'Yes, my voices were from God; they have not deceived me.' Then as she died she cried out 'Jesu!' and was free for ever.

Or is it that of the English King, Charles I? Lord Denning describes his trial as the most memorable in English history.[1]

He was tried in Westminster Hall, London on 20

January, 1649. The King entered the hall dressed in black, relieved only by the Star of the Garter round his neck. When the Roll of Judges was called, sixty-eight responded. The charge was that of treason. The King was accused of being 'a tyrant, traitor, murderer and public and implacable enemy to the Commonwealth of England'. He challenged the authority of the court to charge him and refused to plead. But, despite this, the trial continued. The sentence of the court was 'Charles Steuart Kinge of England...be putt to death by the severinge of his head from his body' and 'executed In the open Streete before Whitehall uppon the morrowe being the thirtieth day of this instante moneth of January.'

In the cold afternoon of that day Charles bravely went to the scaffold. With the help of his executioners he put his long hair under a white satin nightcap and laid down his head on the block. A minute later the executioner held up the severed head with the traditional cry... 'Behold the head of a traitor.'

Or, moving to more modern times, is the most significant trial the Nuremberg trial of Nazi war criminals? The trial was world news and was described by Sir Norman Birkett as 'the greatest trial in history'. Twenty-one Nazis were on trial including the most powerful man in the Third Reich after Hitler, Hermann Goering, along with Rudolf Hess, Joachim von Ribbentrop and others. They represented the Nazi regime. The indictment contained four counts, the first of which charged the defendants with taking part in a common plan or conspiracy to commit crimes against peace, war crimes and crimes against humanity.

The International Tribunal of Judges was composed of judges from the United States, Soviet Russia, Great Britain and France. The President, Lord Justice Lawrence, opened the proceedings by stating:

> The trial which is now about to begin is unique in the history of the jurisprudence of the world and it is of supreme importance to millions of people all over the globe. For these reasons it is laid upon everybody who takes part in this trial a solemn responsibility to discharge their duties without fear or favour, in accordance with the sacred principles of law and justice.

The trial lasted for over two hundred days and at the end only three of the twenty-one defendants were acquitted. All the rest were found guilty on one or more counts in the indictment. Eleven of the defendants were sentenced to death by hanging.

Following the Nuremberg trial there was another dramatic trial, that of the notorious Nazi war criminal Adolf Eichmann. This took place in Jerusalem and, recently, the world has been reminded of this during the trial in Jerusalem of another Nazi, 'Ivan the Terrible'.

Eichmann faced his judges charged with the greatest deliberate slaughter of innocent people in the history of mankind. His prosecutor began the case against him by mentioning the six million victims of the Holocaust. 'Their blood cries to heaven,' he dramatically declared, 'but their voice is not heard. Thus it falls to me to be their mouthpiece.' Despite the evidence against him, Eichmann right to the very end maintained that he was innocent. In an interview with the chaplain assigned by the court to minister to him he stated, 'I did not kill anybody. I am not a murderer. I did not steal, I was not a thief. I am not to blame. Even Jesus Christ would not condemn me.'[2]

But condemned he was. For the first time in the history of the nation of Israel the gallows were used. The sentence of his judges was, 'No one, that is no member of the human race, can be expected to want to share the earth with you. This is the reason, and the only reason, you must hang.'

All these trials had great significance in human history. But was the most significant trial of all time that of Jesus Christ? This, too, took place in Jerusalem and, as in the case of Eichmann, involved both Jews and Gentiles. Jesus, the Jew, was illegally seized by order of the Sanhedrin, then illegally judged, illegally sentenced and illegally killed by a Gentile court. Here was a man who did nothing but good to mankind. By common consent he was the greatest man who has ever lived, but he was condemned to death by a Roman court. So how was it that a trial which broke most of the rules of law resulted in an execution which changed the course of history?

Notes

1. *Leaves from My Library.*
2. William L. Hull, *The Struggle for a Soul* (Doubleday).

1

The Law at the Time of Jesus

The trial of Jesus of Nazareth was one of the most fascinating legal cases of history. It was affected not only by the development of Jewish law, but by the interaction of this law with Roman law. Normally, a crime is judged by the law of the country in which it has been committed. However, at this time Israel was occupied by its enemy, Rome. The Romans allowed the Jews a great deal of freedom; the day-to-day legal matters of the country were carried out by the Jewish courts, but generally only the Roman Governor could sentence someone to death.

At the time of Jesus the main framework of Jewish law was written down in the Pentateuch, the first five books of the Old Testament. This law was developed and extended in the oral (spoken) law. At this time the oral law existed partly of legal traditions which had been handed down from time immemorial and partly of legal decisions which had been made by the courts. All of these were memorised because the Jews considered it to be a religious offence to write them down. But some teachers had private scrolls on which they recorded this oral law for their own use.

The first attempt towards bringing some order and system into this chaotic mass of traditions was made by Hillel, who was President of the Sanhedrin in the time of Herod the Great (40–4 BC).

We have a fair idea of the state of Jewish oral law at the time of Jesus, because in about 200 AD much of the oral law then in existence was collected by Rabbi Judah, a prince, and written down in the *Mishnah*. It was noted for its brevity, clarity and comprehensiveness and was used as a legal text book. Whilst the *Mishnah* may have tended to indicate what the rabbis thought should be the ideal law, rather than the real law that applied at the time, it certainly reflects that law. What cannot be known with certainty is how much this law had changed since the time of Jesus' trial—although probably it was substantially the same. All of this has led to much discussion among scholars about the trial of Jesus and the legal proceedings described in the Gospel accounts. The distinguished legal scholar, Jean Imbert, a professor at Paris University, concludes,

> Nothing in the story of Jesus' trial as presented by the Gospel writers transgresses historical reality. To the contrary, everything given there allows us to maintain that the Gospels were written by men of great intellectual honesty... Far from contradicting themselves, the Evangelists each add certain new elements, and it is only by viewing them all together that one can obtain a comprehensive picture of the different stages of Jesus' trial.[1]

Criminal procedure—then and now

I am glad to say that I have never been arrested. But recently I nearly was! It happened when one of my best friends was, in my opinion, unlawfully arrested by the police. It was Christmas Eve and we had been out to lunch together. As my friend was driving us home he suddenly had a fit and slumped over the steering wheel. With some difficulty I managed to grab the wheel and brought the car to a stop. Just as I did so, a police car drove up. Instead of helping, the police officer quite wrongly jumped to the conclusion that my friend had been drinking, and insisted that he take a breath test. However, my friend, who had not been given time to recover from his fit, was unable to blow the bag properly, and was therefore arrested. Naturally I strongly protested about this. The police officer then threatened to arrest me as well! A few hours later my friend was released with apologies. But it was not a pleasant experience to be arrested on Christmas Eve of all days.

1. The courts

What would have happened to me if I had been unfortunate enough to be arrested for some criminal offence, such as obstructing a police officer? First I would have been charged, then I would have appeared in a magistrate's court. Magistrates in this country are not lawyers, but appear as unpaid judges, receiving only their travelling expenses and a subsistence allowance, and they deal with about ninety-five per cent of all criminal cases. If I had been found guilty in this court, I would then have been able to appeal on a point of law first to the

Crown Court, then the Court of Appeal Criminal Division and eventually, with permission, to the House of Lords.

Under Jewish law most criminal cases were heard by the Lesser Sanhedrin consisting of twenty-three judges. Along with them there were two clerks and two ushers, who also had to administer any necessary scourgings. These courts moved from town to town in the same way as Assize Courts used to do in this country. The highest criminal court was the Great Sanhedrin consisting of seventy-one judges which only met in Jerusalem. This was the Supreme Jewish Court and dealt with serious offences. 'A tribe, a false prophet, or a high priest may not be tried save by the court of one-and-seventy.' [2] The number of judges had remained the same since Moses had appointed seventy elders to aid him in making judgements.[3] The High Priest presided and the court sat in a half-circle so that they could see each other. Two scribes, who were professional lawyers, stood before the judges—one on the right, and one on the left—and they wrote down the arguments of the Accuser and of the Defender.[4]

2. The judges

In English law the majority of criminal cases are heard by lay magistrates, but more serious criminal cases are heard by judges in the Crown Court and by senior judges in the higher courts. As a general rule judges are appointed from the ranks of barristers of at least ten years' standing. The number of judges trying a case is generally limited to three. It would be incredible for an English court to have seventy-one judges. In fact many criminals would maintain that even one judge is one too many!

In the days of Jesus, things were different. The judges of the Sanhedrin were not necessarily lawyers. Some scholars maintain that a 'rabbi' and a 'judge' may be regarded as the same, though the office of judge was voluntary. The qualifications for being a judge were interesting to say the least. 'Not only should the man presenting himself have a fine physique and a splendid command of many languages, he should know all the tricks of sorcerers, and have a mind acute enough to "prove" that the Bible teaches the cleanness of the reptile—which is about as easy, and as useless, as to "prove" the equality of five and seventeen.'[5]

In capital cases involving the death penalty only members of the Sanhedrin who were priests, Levites and Israelites and were able to give their daughters in marriage into the priestly stock were qualified to sit.[6] Because rabbis acted as judges there was a religious background to all court cases. 'A robed clergyman sitting in court judging and penalising speeding motorists would seem strange today—but Judaism integrates what we call the secular into the sacred, and would not consider this in any way foreign to the rabbi's duties.'[7] These judges relied on the professional lawyers (the scribes) for guidance about the law and its procedure. The scribes also acted as Clerks of the Courts.

3. Jurisdiction

In any criminal case it is essential to ascertain whether the court has the right to try the accused.

One famous trial in English law was that in 1945 of William Joyce—better known by his nickname of 'Lord Haw-Haw'. During the Second World War he broadcast Nazi propaganda in English from Germany ('This is Jairmany calling'), warning of the imminent destruction of England. William Joyce was brought to England after the war and in the autumn of 1945 he was tried for treason. The lawyers defending him maintained that the English courts did not have the authority to try him, because his offence had been committed in Germany, and he was not a British subject but an alien. However, William Joyce had lived in this country and was the holder of a British passport. It was held that because of this he owed a duty to the British Crown. He was found guilty of treason and hanged.

The jurisdiction of the Sanhedrin extended not only to the Jews living in Judea, but over the Jewish communities living beyond the Judaean borders. As far as the Gentiles were concerned;

There was apparently only one case in which, if a Roman committed an offence, the Sanhedrin could try the Roman. That was if a person who was not a Jew passed the barrier at the Temple in Jerusalem, beyond which only Jews could go, and thus intruded into the inner Court; he was punished with death, and that even though he were a Roman. Titus referred to this matter in his speech to the Jews during the siege of Jerusalem, when he was trying to save the Temple from destruction; 'Did we not grant you permission to put to death any one who went beyond the barrier, even though he were a Roman?' (*Wars*, VI: ii:4.) But even in such cases the condemnation still required confirmation by the Roman Procurator.[8]

4. Witnesses

In English law criminal proceedings are initiated and carried out mainly by the Crown Prosecution Service. Witnesses have a subordinate role. They can be called either by the prosecution or the defence, they give their evidence under oath and are subject to cross-examination. Important rules govern the way witnesses give evidence; they may not give hearsay evidence and in criminal cases must remain out of court until called to give their evidence. But apart from this they do not play an active part in criminal cases.

In Jewish law witnesses had a unique role. Unlike English law it was the witnesses to a crime who at the beginning of a trial had to initiate the proceedings against the accused. They even had when necessary to assist in carrying out the death sentence. It was essential for there to be two witnesses; 'One witness is not enough to convict a man accused of any crime or offence he may have committed. A matter must be established by the testimony of two or three witnesses.'[9] The accused was brought before the court and, if at least two witnesses corroborated each other about facts which suggested the committing of an offence, a formal charge was then made. It was the task of the scribes as the professional lawyers to formulate the charge indicated by the evidence and to note this in the court records. Until this was done there was no formal accusation or charge before the court and the prisoner was not only deemed to be innocent but unaccused. Certain persons were disqualified from being witnesses. 'Gamblers (habitual dice players) and usurers, and those who bet on the flight of doves; and the merchants who do business with the growth of the sabbatic year.'[10] Also, near relatives could not be witnesses.

The *Mishnah* contains details about how witnesses were to be examined.

> They were brought into separate chambers, and were frightened to tell the truth. They were brought in and warned: 'Perhaps your testimony is based only on a supposition, or on hearsay, or on that of another witness or you have had it from a trustworthy man; or perhaps you are not aware that finally we shall investigate the matter by examination and cross-examination.' After one witness was examined, they let the second enter, and examined him. And if their testimony correspond, the discussion begins with the defence.[11]

5. *The sentence*

In English law the punishment of offenders has four main aims: to deter the offender and others from committing crime; to prevent the offender from committing further crimes (for instance, by taking away his driving licence); to exact retribution to society; to reform the offender by rehabilitation and training. There are various ways in which this is carried out. Even though he has committed a crime the offender can in special circumstances be given an absolute discharge. There is a conditional discharge when a conviction will stand but will be remitted if the offender is of good behaviour for a period of up to three years. Also, there are probation and community service orders. But generally sentences consist of either a fine or imprisonment.

A fine is by far the most usual form of sentence and about eighty per cent of Magistrates' Courts' sentences are fines. Magistrates can impose fines of up to £2,000 and the offender must generally be given time to pay. The most severe sentence is imprisonment itself. Most offences have a fixed maximum prison sentence but usually the offender will receive less than the maximum, possibly serving as little as one-third of his sentence, since he can have up to one-third taken off for parole and one-third for remission. The death sentence (by hanging) was abolished in Britain in 1965.

Jewish law was quite different from English law and under it sentences could take three forms— religious excommunication, corporal punishment and capital punishment. Excommunication was considered to be a worse punishment than corporal punishment, and had three stages. The first stage was *Nezifah* or rebuke, which lasted seven days. The second stage was *Niddui*, which lasted at least for thirty days but not more than sixty. The person in this stage was forbidden to cut his hair or wash his garments, and if he died in disgrace, the local Court of Rabbis was required to stone his coffin—though this became modified to the placing of a stone on the coffin. Failure to make amends then brought the third and more serious stage, *Herem* or anathema. The earlier stages hoped to bring reformation to the offender but the third stage meant that the offender was permanently disgraced.

Corporal punishment was based on Old Testament law. 'When men have a dispute, they are to take it to court and the judges will decide the case, acquitting the innocent and condemning the guilty. If the guilty man deserves to be beaten, the judge shall make him lie down and have him flogged in his presence with the number of lashes his crime deserves, but he must not give him more than forty lashes.'[12] Jewish law amplified this.

The unfortunate prisoner was bent and tied, and these strokes were delivered with the full force of one hand, thirteen on the bared chest, twenty-six on the bared shoulders. It was never intended that this penalty should prove fatal—the flogging was stopped at once on suspicion of danger to life—but of course, accidents did happen, and the scourger was held guiltless unless he had exceeded the sentence.[13]

The most severe sentence was capital punishment. Jewish law carried this out by stoning, burning and decapitation by the sword, depending on the offence committed. Stoning was considered the most severe. The rabbis added a fourth alternative, strangling. They may well have reasoned that this left the body unmutilated for resurrection. Crucifixion was not normally used.

The crimes for which each particular penalty was appropriate were listed exhaustively. Death sentences were very rarely passed and the rabbis tried to minimise the physical sufferings involved. The reluctance of Jewish courts to carry out the death sentence may have been due to the fact that the two chief witnesses for the prosecution were also the two chief executioners and had to assist in carrying out the death sentence. It was laid down that 'The Sanhedrin which condemns to death one man in seven years is accounted murderous.'[14] Rabbi Eleaza Ben Azaria went further and said 'Even one who does so once in seventy years is considered such.' By the time of Jesus it seems likely that the Jews had lost this power, and that only the Roman Governor had the right to sentence someone to death. The restriction on the right of the Jews to do this was important for, otherwise, anyone supporting Rome could be quietly removed by a local execution. It was because of this that the trial of Jesus was transferred to Pilate.[15]

6. Presumption of innocence
In English criminal law the accused is presumed innocent until proved guilty. Also, guilt must be established beyond reasonable doubt; if there is any reasonable doubt as to guilt the accused must be acquitted. The accused is tried on the facts of the case, not on the evidence of previous convictions; the court is not told of the 'record' of the accused save in exceptional circumstances because this might prejudice it. Only if the accused is found guilty will his past record be relevant for sentencing. These safeguards are given to everyone whether they are mass-murderers or litter-bugs. The principle is that it is better for a few guilty people to go free rather than to take the risk of one innocent person being wrongly convicted.

If English law protects the accused, Jewish law did even more so; in fact its great characteristic was that it was framed for the protection of the accused. Until two witnesses had agreed the prisoner was not only presumed to be innocent but unaccused. When there was a case to answer the trial began with the defence. If someone in court said 'I have something to say on behalf of the accused' he was made to join the judges. If the judges thought his evidence was reasonable he was allowed to give it before the court. At the end of a case, if the judges found a good reason to acquit, they did so immediately; and if not they postponed the trial until the next day when the sentence would be given. An acquittal was decided by a majority of one or more judges but condemnation required a majority of at least two. These rules were strictly enforced in cases involving the death sentence.[16]

This was the background of the Jewish law at the time when Jesus of Nazareth came to trial. But before he could be tried, he had to be arrested. And, since he had committed no offence, the people who wished for his death had first to come together in a major conspiracy.

Notes

1. *Le Procés de Jesus* (Presses Universitaires de France).
2. *Mishnah* San. I:5.
3. Numbers 11:16.
4. *Mishnah* San. I:2.
5. Roy A. Stewart, *Judicial Procedure in New Testament Times, Evangelical Quarterly*, Vol 47, p96, 1975.
6. *Mishnah* San. IV:2.

7. Roy A. Stewart, *ibid.*
8. Frank J. Powell, *The Trial of Jesus Christ* (Paternoster Press).
9. Deuteronomy 19:15.
10. *Mishnah* San. III:3, 4.
11. San. III:5, IV:3, V:1.
12. Deuteronomy 25:1–3.
13. Roy A. Stewart, *ibid.*
14. *Tractate Makkoth* 1:10.
15. John 18:31.
16. *Mishnah* San. V:1.

2

The Men Who Plotted Against Jesus

Many of the world's greatest historical figures have been the subjects of plots against their lives. Julius Caesar did not survive the assassination plot led by Brutus. Many ingenious and dangerous assassination plots were carried out against Hitler during the Second World War, but unfortunately they all failed. In England, the most famous plot is probably the so-called Gunpowder Plot. It was led by the Roman Catholic Yorkshire soldier, Guy Fawkes, who planned to blow up the House of Lords on 5 November, 1605, when the King, James I, would be present at the opening of Parliament. But Guy Fawkes was betrayed and he was found in the cellar of the House of Lords with thirty-six barrels of gunpowder. He and his conspirators were arrested and executed. Ever since then the Gunpowder Plot has been commemorated by bonfires on 5 November.

The Gunpowder Plot failed but the conspiracy against Jesus succeeded. It is obvious that from the very beginning of his ministry the authorities were out to get Jesus. It comes as quite a shock to find Mark in the beginning of his Gospel recording,

'Then the Pharisees went out and began to plot with the Herodians how they might kill Jesus.'[1] Who was it who conspired against Jesus and why?

The Pharisees

These are often associated with the scribes, but strictly speaking they were not the same. The scribes could be said to be the lawyers of their day. The main interest of the Pharisees was the law and so they and the scribes had much in common. Often they acted together as in the case of Jesus.

The Pharisees became a distinct group in the second century BC. They respected and loved all the law, but especially the spoken (oral) law, which was recorded by the scribes. The attitude of the Pharisees to the law interests me as a lawyer. I have been practising law for forty years and it has become part of my life. But any respect that I have for the law is nothing compared to that of the Pharisees. I have found that very often the law is fallible but to them it was given by God. They even believed that the law was created two thousand years before the world was created and it would last after the world came to an end. They had a saying, 'There are twelve hours in the day and during the first three the Holy One sits down and occupies himself with the law.' To them every jot and tittle of the law was inspired and given by God.

The results of this were staggering. During my career I have studied many Acts of Parliament and read cases in the Law Reports. Certainly, English law is much more complicated than it used to be and at times hard to understand, but any difficulties in interpreting English law are mild compared with those of the Pharisees in interpreting God's law. Because they believed that the law was final and complete, it had to cover the whole of life. Thus the moral principles contained in the Ten Commandments were turned into an infinity of petty rules and regulations.

For example, the Pharisees had to interpret the fourth commandment, 'Observe the Sabbath day by keeping it holy, as the Lord your God has commanded you. Six days you shall labour and do all your work, but the seventh day is a Sabbath to the Lord your God. On it you shall not do any work, neither you, nor your son or daughter, nor your manservant or maidservant, nor your ox, your donkey or any of your animals, nor the alien within your gates.'[2] From this simple commandment there arose scores of rules and regulations contained in twenty-four chapters of the Jewish *Mishnah*. These deal with what work is and then go on to define what constitutes a burden, which could not be carried on the Sabbath. For instance, one could only carry milk enough for a gulp, honey enough to put on a sore, ink enough to write two letters of the alphabet, a pebble big enough to throw at a bird, and so on. While it was the scribes who worked out all these rules and regulations it was the Pharisees who devoted their whole lives to keeping them. The result was no doubt good for the lawyers of those days, but a complete nightmare to the ordinary people who had to keep these rules and regulations.

But we must not think that the Pharisees were basically bad. They were religious men and in some ways the best men of their race at that time. They were the teachers and guardians of the law. They ran the schools and the synagogues and were men of a high moral character. Professor F.F. Bruce has pointed out, 'The reader of the Gospels is sometimes surprised to be told that the party with which Jesus had most in common was the Pharisees. How comes it, then, he may ask, that Jesus and the Pharisees appear to have been involved in controversy every time they crossed each other's path?'[3] How, indeed, did these most religious and law-abiding citizens come to be involved in an illegal plot to kill Jesus?

The Pharisees were angered by many things. They were made furious by the authority with which Jesus spoke, and which runs throughout all his teaching. One of his characteristic sayings was 'I tell you.' The Pharisees spoke *from* authority but Jesus spoke *with* authority. 'The people were amazed at his teaching, because he taught them as one who had authority, not as a teacher of the law.'[4] This was deeply resented by the Pharisees. After all, they were the ones who had given their lives to the interpretation of the law. Who was this upstart? What right had a carpenter from Nazareth to teach like this?

Jesus was popular with the crowd and taught that God's love included everyone. Sadly, the Pharisees were proud of their position and deeply resented the universal appeal of Jesus. Down the ages good religious men have often become like them. Their attitude is well summed up in four lines of doggerel:

We are God's chosen few,
All others will be damned;
There is no room in heaven for you—
We can't have heaven crammed.

Also, Jesus was indifferent to their interpretation of the law. To Jesus the spirit of the law was far greater than the letter. In particular, the Pharisees resented the apparent disregard of Jesus for their interpretation of the laws relating to the Sabbath. When Jesus healed on the Sabbath a man who had been paralysed for thirty-eight years there were protests. 'Because Jesus was doing these things on the Sabbath, the Jews persecuted him.'[5] Matters became worse when the disciples of Jesus were hungry and plucked and ate ears of corn as they passed through the cornfields on the Sabbath day. 'When the Pharisees saw this, they said to him, "Look! Your disciples are doing what is unlawful on the Sabbath." '[6] Jesus replied not only by giving the example of David and his followers, who when they were hungry ate the consecrated bread, but he went on to say 'The Son of Man is Lord of the Sabbath.' The result was that 'The Pharisees went out and plotted how they might kill Jesus.'[7]

Finally, they were furious with Jesus because of his attacks upon them. Jesus was certainly not 'meek and mild' in our modern sense of the words. He spoke some of the harshest words that have ever been spoken, and usually against the Pharisees. Time after time he exposed their hypocrisy. In Matthew's Gospel we find Jesus saying seven times 'Woe to you, teachers of the law and Pharisees, you hypocrites!' He then accuses them of shutting the kingdom of

30

heaven in men's faces, making their converts twice as much sons of hell as they are, breaking their oaths, neglecting the law, being full of greed and like white-washed tombs! He then ends his denunciation by saying 'You snakes! You brood of vipers! How will you escape being condemned to hell?'[8] No wonder Jesus was not popular with the Pharisees and they were angry with him. It never occurred to them that these words might be true. For them the only solution was to end this nuisance once and for all by killing Jesus.

The Sadducees

We do not know how the word 'Sadducee' was derived. Some scholars think that it came from the name of Zadok, a priest during the time of David and Solomon. Whether this is so or not, this group as a Jewish party began about two hundred years before the birth of Jesus.

The Sadducees were the aristocrats of the Jews. Their head was the High Priest and they were a small select group wielding great power. When Palestine became part of the Roman Empire the Sadducees co-operated with the Romans, in order to preserve their wealth and privileged position. While the Pharisees and Sadducees are often mentioned together in the New Testament, they were different from each other, and the beliefs of the two groups were nearly opposite. The Pharisees believed in the resurrection of the dead and a day of judgement to come. The Sadducees did not.

Another basic difference between the Sadducees

and the Pharisees was their attitude to the law. As already mentioned, the Pharisees considered the scribal or oral law to be all-important. The Sadducees rejected this and accepted only what was written in the Pentateuch, the first five books of the Bible. They had no time for the masses of rules and regulations on which the Pharisees founded their religion. Again, this led to conflict.

In view of their differences, why is it that the Sadducees were just as eager as the Pharisees in plotting the death of Jesus? This was for political motives. They thought that Jesus was a revolutionary about to organise a rebellion against Rome. This would be the end of their privileged position. It could not be allowed even if it meant that Jesus had to be put to death. William Barclay well summarises the position;

> The Pharisees hated Jesus from religious motives, even if these motives were entirely mistaken. The Sadducees hated Jesus for no other reason than worldly and materialistic selfishness. To ensure their own continued comfort and luxury the Sadducees were prepared to do anything to obliterate this perilous and disturbing Jesus of Nazareth.[9]

In particular two actions of Jesus aroused the wrath of the Sadducees. The first was when he cleansed the temple. When he came to Jerusalem he found that its outer courts were used as a cattle market and a place for the changing of money. It was more like an oriental bazaar than the house of God. This was done with the permission of the Sadducees who no doubt took a 'rake-off' for themselves. They turned a blind eye to the way in which the poor were fleeced, while they themselves lived in luxury. But Jesus 'made a whip out of cords, and drove all from the temple area, both sheep and cattle; he scattered the coins of the money changers and overturned their tables. To those who sold doves he said, "Get these out of here! How dare you turn my Father's house into a market!" '[10] The Sadducees could not overlook this. After all, their trade was threatened.

The second thing that Jesus did was to raise Lazarus from the dead. As far as the Sadducees were concerned this was the 'last straw'. According to them there was no resurrection. Imagine how they must have felt when they heard that Lazarus had been raised from the dead! The Sadducees called the first of four meetings of the Sanhedrin, and joined with the Pharisees to plot how to kill Jesus. From that moment onwards the die was cast.

The Herodians

As their name implies this party supported the family of Herod. The founder of this was Herod the Great, but it is certainly a misnomer to call him 'the Great'. He was appointed King of Judea by the Roman Senate in 40 BC and gained control in 37 BC. Loyal to Rome, his rule was a time of material progress but of misery for his subjects. The Jewish historian Josephus said that he was the most cruel tyrant who ever ascended the throne. Josephus mentions the vast number of people he killed and tortured.

During his rule hardly a day passed without someone being sentenced to death. He was ruthless, murdering his wife, three of his sons, his mother-in-law, brother-in-law, uncle and many others—not to mention the babies born at Bethlehem around the time of the birth of Jesus. There was a famous saying about him that it was better to be Herod's pig than his son! After his death, during Jesus' lifetime, his kingdom was divided among three of his sons. One of them, Herod Antipas, was Tetrarch of Galilee. Jesus came from Galilee and so the Herodians there regarded him and his disciples as a threat to their ruler. Again, we find two Jewish parties that have little in common, the Herodians and the Pharisees, plotting to kill Jesus. However, the Herodians evidently had religious as well as political interests, and some have identified them with the Essenes, to whom Herod the Great showed special favour.

After Jesus went to his local synagogue and healed the man with the shrivelled hand Mark records, 'Then the Pharisees went out and began to plot with the Herodians how they might kill Jesus.'[11] Subsequent to this the Pharisees and the Herodians tried to trap Jesus with a trick question about whether it was lawful to pay taxes to Caesar. Jesus gave his famous reply, ' "Why are you trying to trap me?" he asked. "Bring me a denarius and let me look at it." They brought the coin, and he asked them, "Whose portrait is this? And whose inscription?" "Caesar's," they replied. Then Jesus said to them, "Give to Caesar what is Caesar's and to God what is God's." '[12] At that time this so amazed them that they left Jesus and went away, but the respite was only temporary. More was to come. Eventually Jesus appeared on trial before Herod Antipas before he met his final fate.

And so these three groups, each for their own reasons, came together in a final attempt to finish once and for all this threat to their own positions. Their motives were varied. These were religious, economic, political and personal. But one belief united them. Jesus was a menace and must be killed.

Notes

1. Mark 3:6.
2. Deuteronomy 5:12–14.
3. *The Real Jesus* (Hodder and Stoughton).
4. Mark 1:22.
5. John 5:16.
6. Matthew 12:2.
7. Matthew 12:8, 14.
8. Matthew 23:1–33.
9. *The Mind of Jesus* (SCM Press).
10. John 2:15, 16.
11. Mark 3:6.
12. Mark 12:13–17.

3

The Plot

The plot to kill Jesus had been building up since the very beginning of his ministry.

1. Healing on the Sabbath
The Gospels record that the plot to kill Jesus was started by the Pharisees and the Herodians, after Jesus had healed a man with a paralysed hand, and had declared that 'The Sabbath was made for man, not man for the Sabbath. So the Son of Man is Lord even of the Sabbath.'[1] The Pharisees were not concerned about the healing but were angry about it taking place on the Sabbath, and so they 'went out and began to plot with the Herodians how they might kill Jesus'.[2]

2. The Feast of the Tabernacles
During the months that followed the plot to kill Jesus gained support. One year later it came to a head at the time of the Feast of the Tabernacles. This great feast celebrated the completion of harvest and commemorated God's goodness to the Jewish people during their wanderings in the desert. Up to this time Jesus had confined his ministry to Galilee and had

stayed away from Jerusalem because he knew that the Jews there were waiting to take his life, but halfway through the feast he went to Jerusalem and began to teach. 'The Jews were amazed and asked, "How did this man get such learning without having studied?" Jesus answered, "My teaching is not my own. It comes from him who sent me." '[3]

This claim of Jesus that his teaching was from God had a dramatic effect on the crowds who had assembled for the feast. They had never heard anything like it. Some accused him of being demon-possessed. Others were puzzled. Yet others wondered if he were the Christ, the long-awaited Messiah. 'The Pharisees heard the crowd whispering such things about him. Then the chief priest and the Pharisees sent temple guards to arrest him.'[4] But this attempt failed. Not only did the crowd prevent it but 'Finally the temple guards went back to the chief priests and Pharisees, who asked them, "Why didn't you bring him in?" "No-one ever spoke the way this man does," the guards declared. "You mean he has deceived you also?" the Pharisees retorted.'[5]

3. *Accusations of blasphemy*
This was not the end of the matter. The next attempt on Jesus' life was shortly after the feast had ended, when the crowd who had come for the feast had gone home. Jesus remained in Jerusalem, giving the Pharisees an opportunity to challenge and cross-question him. As they did so the opposition to him intensified. The Jews accused Jesus of being demon-possessed. Jesus replied, 'I am not possessed by a demon but I honour my Father and you dishonour me.' The Jews

retorted, 'Who do you think you are?' Jesus replied, ' "Your father Abraham rejoiced at the thought of seeing my day; he saw it and was glad." "You are not yet fifty years old," the Jews said to him, "and you have seen Abraham!" "I tell you the truth," Jesus answered, "before Abraham was born, I am!" At this, they picked up stones to stone him, but Jesus hid himself, slipping away from the temple grounds.'[6] These words of Jesus, 'I am!', were interpreted by the Jews as nothing less than blasphemy. The name 'I AM' was used by God in the Old Testament to refer to himself. This was quite monstrous. The punishment for this offence was death by stoning. The law was quite clear. 'Anyone who blasphemes the name of the Lord must be put to death. The entire assembly must stone him. Whether an alien or native-born, when he blasphemes the Name, he must be put to death.'[7]

4. The Feast of Dedication

The next attempt to kill Jesus was in winter, at the Feast of Dedication, about two months after the first attempt. The Feast of Dedication dated from the time of Judas Maccabaeus (165 BC) when the temple was cleansed after it had been profaned. It was a time of celebration and during its eight days no one was allowed to weep or fast. Every householder was required to light at least one candle. The greater the illumination the better. If there were ten persons in a house there must be ten candles the first night, and the number must be increased each night until the eighth when there were to be eighty.

At this feast Jesus was urged by the Jews to plainly

declare who he was. They 'gathered around him, saying, "How long will you keep us in suspense? If you are the Christ, tell us plainly." ' Jesus answered this challenge by claiming that not only was God his Father, but that ' "I and the Father are one." Again the Jews picked up stones to stone him, but Jesus said to them, "I have shown you many great miracles from the Father. For which of these do you stone me?" "We are not stoning you for any of these," replied the Jews, "but for blasphemy, because you, a mere man, claim to be God." '8

5. *The first meeting of the Sanhedrin*

So the plot against Jesus gathered momentum. It was no longer safe for him to remain in Jerusalem and he retired beyond Jordan. But in the meantime the hostility of the chief priests and Pharisees continued to grow. At all costs Jesus had to be arrested and sentenced to death. The supreme court of the Jews, the Sanhedrin, now became involved.

An informal meeting was called to discuss the situation after Jesus had raised Lazarus from the dead. The situation was urgent. By now Jesus was so popular that the great fear was that the people would make him a king. Caiaphas, the High Priest and a Sadducee, more or less presided, and took the lead in opposing Jesus. The Pharisees, who had laid the foundation for the opposition, now withdrew into the background. There was much debate. Some decisive steps had to be taken.

'If we let him go on like this, everyone will believe in him, and then the Romans will come and take away both our place and our nation.'9 The members of the Sanhedrin were perplexed. But most of them hesitated to propose what would amount to judicial murder, until Caiaphas spoke up in his blunt way. He threw a different light on the situation. 'You do not realise that it is better for you that one man die for the people than that the whole nation perish.'[10]

The point was taken. The duty of the Sanhedrin was now plain. Here was a way in which the members of the Sanhedrin could reconcile judicial murder with their own consciences; even see it as their duty. Jesus had to be killed. If he was allowed to live, the whole nation would perish but if he were to die, the nation would be saved. John goes on to record, 'So from that day on they plotted to take his life. Therefore Jesus no longer moved about publicly among the Jews. Instead he withdrew to a region near the desert, to a village called Ephraim, where he stayed with his disciples.'[11]

But it was one thing to have resolved to arrest Jesus and another thing to actually effect the arrest. Jesus now appeared on the 'Wanted List' of the Jews. Notices about him were probably distributed, and from the Talmud and the New Testament we can reconstruct what they might have said:

WANTED: YESHU HANNOSRI

He shall be stoned because he has practised sorcery and enticed Israel to apostasy. Anyone who can say anything in his favour let him come forward and plead on his behalf. Anyone who knows where he is, let him declare it to the Great Sanhedrin in Jerusalem.[12]

Orders were also given out by the chief priests and

Pharisees that if anyone found out where Jesus was he should report it. Failure to do this would have been a criminal offence.

6. *The second meeting of the Sanhedrin*

This was held on the Wednesday before the Passover, and was probably an adjournment of the previous meeting. Matters had now come to a head. Jesus had come up to Jerusalem for the Passover and had made his triumphal entry a few days earlier. The chief priests, scribes and elders met in Caiaphas' palace. 'They plotted to arrest Jesus in some sly way and kill him. "But not during the Feast," they said, "or there may be a riot among the people." '[13] The authorities were on the horns of a dilemma. To arrest Jesus at the time of the Passover could lead to a riot. On the other hand, his popularity was growing and already there had been a large demonstration in his favour. What were they to do? As they debated this, much to their relief a messenger announced that one of the disciples of Jesus, Judas Iscariot, had approached the temple guard and was demanding an interview with the council.

Judas was introduced, and, standing before the council, explained that, being one of the Twelve, he was well acquainted with all Jesus' movements. He was thus in a unique position to guide the temple guard to a spot where Jesus could be arrested when alone and unprotected. He wanted a price for this service, namely thirty pieces of silver. This offer was too good to be refused. It afforded an opportunity that might never occur again. The council quickly agreed to it and gave Judas there and then his thirty pieces of silver. Matthew records, 'From then on Judas watched for an opportunity to hand him over.'[14] The arrest of Jesus was imminent.

Notes

1. Mark 2:27.
2. Mark 3:6.
3. John 7:15, 16.
4. John 7:32.
5. John 7:45–47.
6. John 8:56–59.
7. Leviticus 24:16.
8. John 10:24, 30–33.
9. John 11:48.
10. John 11:50.
11. John 11:53, 54.
12. Paul Maier, *First Easter* (Harper and Row).
13. Matthew 26:4, 5.
14. Matthew 26:16.

4

Arrest

The records of the trial of Jesus found in the Gospels agree in a remarkable way.[1] We can use them to follow Jesus through his arrest and trial, or rather trials. Normally, in Jewish as in English law, someone suspected of a serious offence would be arrested, then charged and then tried. However, the circumstances behind Jesus' arrest were unusual. Most people try to avoid being arrested; Jesus was different. He knew that Judas was going to betray him. Yet he went to the Garden of Gethsemane; a favourite meeting place of Jesus and the disciples. Judas, after slipping out of the upper room during the Last Supper on an ostensibly innocent mission, went to the Jewish authorities. He reported to them not only that Jesus and his disciples had gone to the Garden of Gethsemane but, above all, that Jesus was talking about his own death. Now was the hour to strike. But there were complications. The Passover festival began the next day. Was there time for Jesus to be arrested, tried and executed before then? To hold him as a prisoner over the festival period was too dangerous. A few days earlier Jesus had been hailed by a great crowd of people as 'The king who comes in the name of the Lord!'[2] An attempt to rescue him could not be ruled out. To use a legal phrase, 'Time was of the essence of the contract.'

Realising this, the Jewish authorities made thorough preparations. In all probability Caiaphas, the High Priest, consulted with the Roman Governor, Pontius Pilate, as to whether he would hear this case on the next day and endorse the finding of the Jewish court. A formidable arrest party was then assembled. This included the chief priests, the temple guard, a detachment of Roman soldiers and a great crowd armed with swords and cudgels and carrying torches and lanterns.[3] Altogether more than a hundred men were involved. This may seem an excessive force to arrest just one man. But the authorities remembered to their cost how on a previous occasion the temple guards had failed to arrest Jesus.[4] They may well have feared a riot. It was, probably, for this reason that a detachment of Roman soldiers was involved. It would act as a back-up for the Jewish guard. Nothing was being left to chance. The arrest party was prepared for trouble and fully armed to meet it. The torches and lanterns show that it anticipated having to search for Jesus in the recesses of the garden.

As things turned out, there was no need for this display of force. When the arrest party arrived at the garden it was essential for Jesus to be picked out from the disciples. By then it was dark and this could have been difficult. Judas had arranged with the chief priests and elders to identify Jesus by giving him a kiss. In those days kissing was a common form

44

of greeting and it would not arouse suspicion on the part of the disciples. As soon as they got to the garden Judas, as arranged, identified Jesus by kissing him. Jesus, however, knew immediately what he was doing and asked him, 'Judas, are you betraying the Son of Man with a kiss?' Then 'Jesus, knowing all that was going to happen to him, went out and asked them, "Who is it you want?" "Jesus of Nazareth," they replied. "I am he," Jesus said.'[5] Again, the use of the words 'I am' could have been a claim by Jesus that he was God. But whether this was the case or not, the effect was startling enough. The arrest party found themselves confronted by a commanding figure, who so far from running away came out to meet them. This produced a moment of terror or awe, and the party retreated and fell back in confusion. They had expected resistance. Both the action and words of Jesus together with his calm control of events caught them by surprise.

Jesus then once again asked, 'Who is it you want?' and they said, 'Jesus of Nazareth.' Jesus answered, 'I told you that I am he.' He then asked the soldiers to let his disciples go. The arrest party was not interested in them. He was the one that they had come to arrest. At this moment Peter, in a typical action, drew his sword to defend Jesus and cut off the right ear of the High Priest's servant, Malchus. Jesus immediately intervened. 'Put your sword away.' He rejected resistance in this way. Luke, the doctor, then records that Jesus touched the ear of Malchus and healed him.[6] This rejection of force inevitably led to the arrest of Jesus. 'The detachment of soldiers with its commander and the Jewish officials arrested

Jesus. They bound him and brought him first to Annas.'[7]

As Jesus was led away, we get the impression that they were not taking him, but he was freely giving himself up. Throughout his arrest Jesus was completely master of the situation. The initiative was always with him.

Notes

1. See Appendix.
2. Luke 19:38.
3. Luke 22:52; John 18:3.
4. John 7:32, 44.
5. Luke 22:48; John 18:4, 5.
6. Luke 22:51.
7. John 18:12, 13.

5

The Jewish Trial

The trial of Jesus was unique in many ways. Normally, in Jewish law, witnesses acted as prosecutors and their duty was to bring a charge against the accused; this would be a clear statement of the offence alleged together with evidence to support it. Instead, the decision to arrest Jesus was taken by the authorities, and at no stage in the proceedings against him was Jesus formally charged with any offence. In fact, he was eventually sentenced not for any offence which happened before he went to court but for something which happened in the court itself. Imagine the hue and cry there would be today if a man was on trial for his life, but at no stage in the proceedings was he ever charged with any offence! Unbelievably, it was his judges who conspired to have Jesus convicted.

Another unique thing about the trial of Jesus is the number of times he appeared in court. In fact, it is more correct to speak of the trials, rather than the trial, of Jesus. Never has anyone been tried by so many courts in such a short space of time. Within about ten hours Jesus appeared six times before four different judges. His main trials were those before the Jews and the Romans, each of which had three separate stages. As Lord Shaw of Dunfermline has pointed out, 'Jesus Christ underwent a double trial. Two great and independent systems of criminal jurisprudence were called into play to determine his fate.'[1]

The examination before Annas

After Jesus had been arrested, John tells us that 'They bound him and brought him first to Annas, who was the father-in-law of Caiaphas, the high priest that year.'[2] There is nothing surprising in Jesus being brought before Annas rather than Caiaphas. He was the head of the family and, by Jewish law, still High Priest. His house was probably on the way from the Garden of Gethsemene to the Roman fortress the Tower of Antonia. Furthermore, the house of Annas derived much of its wealth from the business side of the temple. Jesus had just overturned the temple stalls, which were the property of Annas and his family. No doubt Annas used his influence to arrange that Jesus should be brought to him to answer for this.

In English law every criminal case must first be heard before local magistrates. They can either then deal with the case themselves or, in more serious cases, commit the accused to be tried in the Crown Court. In these cases the function of the magistrates is to see whether there is a *prima facie* case against the accused and to weed out prosecutions that have no real chance of success. While Jewish law is different, the examination of Jesus before Annas appears to have been a preliminary examination. Strictly speaking this was illegal, for Jewish law provided strict safeguards for the accused, in that he could not be asked about his offence until formally charged. As William Barclay has pointed out, 'One curious feature of legal procedure in the Sanhedrin was that the man involved was held to be absolutely innocent, and, indeed, not even on trial, until the evidence of the witnesses had been stated and confirmed. The argument about the case could only begin when the testimony of the witnesses was given and confirmed.'[3]

Bearing this in mind we can see how this examination before Annas proceeded. Annas began by questioning Jesus about his disciples and his teaching. Perhaps he wished to insinuate that Jesus and the disciples were revolutionaries plotting against the existing government. Jesus, in his reply, does not mention the disciples. He is clearly determined to protect them. For himself he replies, 'I always taught in synagogues or at the temple, where all the Jews come together. I said nothing in secret. Why question me? Ask those who heard me. Surely they know what I said.' In other words, Jesus is saying, 'There is no case to answer. Ask the witnesses for yourself.' William Barclay comments, 'That is the point of the conversation between Jesus and Annas. Jesus in that incident was reminding Annas that he had no right to ask him anything until the evidence of witnesses had been taken and found to agree.'

John records, 'When Jesus said this, one of the officials near by struck him in the face. ' "Is that any way to answer the high priest?" he demanded.'[4] This assault was quite illegal, but it should not surprise us. The whole of these proceedings was tainted with illegality. Jesus then defends himself by inviting this man to give evidence of any evil that he has spoken. 'If I spoke amiss, state this in evidence.'[5]

At this stage Annas quite wrongly concluded that there was a sufficient case to bring Jesus on trial before Caiaphas the High Priest. The preliminary examination, inadequate as it was, had ended. 'Then Annas sent him, still bound, to Caiaphas the high priest.'[6]

The trial before Caiaphas and the Sanhedrin

Caiaphas was the son-in-law of Annas, the current High Priest and thus the most important man in the Jewish state. In a unique way he was not only the religious leader of the Jews but also their political and judicial head. Just as during the Roman occupation the Procurator represented the Roman State, so the High Priest represented the Jewish State. As such he was responsible to the Roman Procurator for the good order and discipline of the Jews.

Josephus (writing in the first century AD) gives us details of the origin of this high office.

> History informs us that Aaron, the brother of Moses, officiated to God as a High Priest, and that, after his death, his sons succeeded him immediately; and that this dignity hath been continued down from them all to their posterity. Whence it is the custom of our country, that no one should take the high priesthood of God, but he who is the blood of Aaron, while everyone that is of

50

another stock, though he were king, can never obtain that high priesthood.

The High Priest was the supreme judge in Israel. Just as Moses presided over the seventy elders so the High Priest presided over the Greater Sanhedrin of seventy. No one in Israel was allowed to disobey the orders of the High Priest. His authority was supreme and could not be denied. In the time of Jesus the office of High Priest was in the hands of the Sadducees, who were behind the arrest of Jesus. It was therefore unlikely from the start that Jesus would have a fair trial, and the records confirm this.

Amongst scholars there has been much debate as to whether this trial before Caiaphas took place at a formal session of the Sanhedrin or, like the appearance before Annas, was merely a preliminary enquiry. Mark's Gospel records that 'They took Jesus to the high priest, and all the other chief priests, elders and teachers of the law came together... The chief priests and the whole Sanhedrin were looking for evidence against Jesus.'[7] This sounds like a formal Jewish trial, but because of the breaches of the law as laid down in the *Mishnah* some scholars have argued that this could not have been a formal trial. But there are other trials reported from this time in which the authorities played fast and loose with the law, such as the stoning of Stephen[8] and the attempted stoning of the woman taken in adultery,[9] so this may represent a breakdown in Jewish law under Roman occupation.

In Jewish law it was usual for the trial to follow at once after the arrest. Because of this, and the approaching Passover, there was no time to take Jesus to the Palace of Caiaphas, and the trial took place in an upper room in his house, at night-time. This was also illegal because according to Jewish law no case involving the death sentence should be tried at night.

The trial began with the taking of evidence which is essential to any legal case. First, Matthew records that 'The chief priests and the whole Sanhedrin were looking for false evidence against Jesus so that they could put him to death. But they did not find any, though many false witnesses came forward.'[10] Mark adds to this 'Their statements did not agree.'[11] By doing this, Caiaphas and the Sanhedrin were guilty of three breaches of the law. First, they should not have been looking for witnesses. As judges they should not only have been neutral but should have acted as Counsel for the Defence. They should have left the business of providing witnesses to others and not have taken it on themselves. Then, to make matters worse, they were looking for false witnesses. It was bad enough to seek for witnesses at all; but to seek for false evidence compounded the matter. Lastly, they were directly seeking to put Jesus to death. This was absolutely illegal. In a case involving the death sentence they should have been even more on the side of the accused. Instead, the fate of Jesus was sealed before he was even tried. Clearly, Annas and Caiaphas had organised the whole process; they were far more responsible for the death of Jesus than either Judas or Pilate. Despite all this they could not find even two false witnesses to agree. In Jewish law this was called 'vain testimony'. The evidence of the witnesses did not agree. It could not even be accepted provisionally. Jesus was unaccused, and the trial should have been abandoned.

But this was not the end of the trial. Matthew records that finally two witnesses came forward and declared, 'This fellow said, "I am able to destroy the temple of God and rebuild it in three days." '[12] We do not know who these further two witnesses were, though it has been suggested that they were connected with the temple police. Then, at long last a charge was made against Jesus. He was accused of sacrilege of the worst kind. To the Jews the temple was the dwelling-place of God. Nothing could be worse than its destruction. To speak in these terms was to blaspheme the temple; and to blaspheme the temple was to blaspheme God himself. To the crime of sacrilege was added that of blasphemy and also that of sorcery, for it was presumed that only by Satanic power could a man rebuild in three days the temple of God which had taken forty-six years to build. These charges were indeed serious. Also, as Professor Bruce points out, they had deep implications.

As a concession to Jewish religious sentiment there was one area in which the Roman administration allowed the Sanhedrin to exercise unrestricted authority; this was the area of offences against the sanctity of the temple... If this evidence had been admissible, there would have been a *prima facie* case for the court to go ahead and deal with the charge in its own authority, without any reference to the Roman Governor.[13]

Jewish law in its *Hakiroth* (searching queries) gives

seven questions which must be asked of a witness in a trial for blasphemy, which relate to the time and place of the blasphemy. These two witnesses would easily be able to answer these questions. The occasion on which Jesus was meant to have said these words was about two years earlier on the first cleansing of the temple. John records his exact words; 'Destroy this temple, and I will raise it again in three days,' but John then adds, 'But the temple he had spoken of was his body.'[14] These two witnesses had twisted the words of Jesus and by a wilful misrepresentation tried to make them say something which he had not said. No wonder Mark records 'Yet even then their testimony did not agree.'[15] For the second time the prosecution had failed. There was no case before the court. Once again Jesus was unaccused.

At this stage in the proceedings there was another illegality. According to Jewish law the Sanhedrin should now have dealt with these false witnesses. Their testimony did not agree and Moses wrote, 'The judges must make a thorough investigation, and if the witness proves to be a liar, giving false testimony against his brother, then do to him as he intended to do to his brother.'[16] These witnesses had tried to swear a man's life away; and their own lives should have been forfeited. While we are not told what happened to them it is more than likely that they did not pay any penalty, let alone what was laid down by the law. Caiaphas and the Sanhedrin protected them.

By now one thing was quite certain. The case against Jesus had broken down. Twice witnesses had disagreed. Jesus was still unaccused. The trial, if there ever was one, should have ended. But Caiaphas was determined to have Jesus convicted and condemned to death. Instead of discharging him he now stood up and cross-examined Jesus. He ignored the fact that the only two witnesses had failed to agree. ' "Are you not going to answer? What is this testimony that these men are bringing against you?" But Jesus remained silent and gave no answer.'[17] Jesus was quite entitled to remain silent. Not only was he unaccused but, even if he had been, Jewish law like English law gave an accused the right of silence. No one could be compelled to convict themselves by being forced to speak.

This silence of Jesus must have infuriated Caiaphas more than ever. He now threw all semblance of legality to the winds. Something happened which is unique in legal history. Caiaphas ceased to be a judge and turned himself into Counsel for the Prosecution, taking the case into his own hands. What had started out as a trial now became an inquisition. Matthew tells us how Caiaphas put Jesus on oath and used the Oath of Testimony ('I charge you by the living God'), despite the fact that it was illegal to do this in a trial for life. By Jewish law Jesus had to reply. In this case, silence would have been by itself an admission of guilt. The climax of the trial had been reached.

'Are you the Christ, the Son of the Blessed One?'[18] asked Caiaphas. As Jesus replied, he knew that he was signing his own death warrant. ' "I am," said Jesus. "And you will see the Son of Man sitting at the right hand of the Mighty One and coming on the clouds of heaven." '[19] Jesus gave Caiaphas all that he wished for and more. In reply to the question, 'Are you the Christ?', Jesus said emphatically 'I am'. Yes, he was the Messiah, the Son of God. But he added to this. He was the one who would sit at the right hand of God. He was the one who would come on the clouds of heaven. Caiaphas and the Sanhedrin regarded themselves as his judges but the day was coming when he would judge them! Professor F.F. Bruce explains the significance of this reply:

> The judges could scarcely believe their ears. The accused man, they reckoned, had convicted himself out of his own mouth. No need of further witnesses: this was plain blasphemy, and they had heard it for themselves. In later codifications of Jewish law, blasphemy was limited to the pronouncement of the unutterable name of the God of Israel (the name spelt with the four consonants YHWH). There is no suggestion that Jesus pronounced this name, but his language, to those who grasped its purport, implied that he was the assessor and peer of the Most High. If this did not amount to constructive blasphemy, it is difficult to imagine what did count as such. If Jesus had contented himself with claiming to be the Messiah, the Pharisaic members of the court might have deplored his claim but they would not have regarded it as ground for a severe sentence and they would probably not have been happy about handing him over to the Romans. But his additional words altered the situation. It was not safe for the city or the nation to let such a 'blasphemer' go free; God would not hold them guiltless if they took no steps to restrain him.[20]

When Jesus made the claim that he was the Son of God Caiaphas the High Priest tore his clothes. This was a sign of great grief or shock. By the law of Moses the High Priest was forbidden to tear his garments even when mourning for the dead. But when acting as judge he was required by custom to express in this way his horror of any blasphemy uttered in his presence. Jesus had now incriminated himself. 'You have heard the blasphemy,' said Caiaphas, 'What do you think?' There was only one answer. The verdict was unanimous. 'They all condemned him as worthy of death.'[21] Once Jesus was condemned the Sanhedrin showed its contempt of his apparently monstrous behaviour. 'Some began to spit at him; they blindfolded him, struck him with their fists, and said "Prophesy!" And the guards took him and beat him.'[22] The reference to blindfolding could tie up with an ancient prophecy that when the Messiah comes he will be able to judge by smell without the need of sight. In other words, the members of the Sanhedrin were saying, 'If you are really the Messiah show us by "prophesying" who it was that struck you.' So, by bending the rules of law in every conceivable direction, Caiaphas had got his own way. Jesus had been condemned to death.

The second trial before the Sanhedrin

The trial by night was over. But because, under Jewish law, no case involving the death sentence could be tried at night, it was now necessary to re-assemble the whole Sanhedrin early in the morning to ratify what had already taken place. There was no time to lose. Caiaphas had to make sure that no conscientious member of the Sanhedrin raised an objection about the previous night's proceedings. Also, it was necessary to obtain a death-warrant from Pilate, for the Jewish court did not have the power to carry out the death sentence. We are not certain as to whether a larger number of judges now re-assembled, but probably this was the case. Luke in his Gospel gives the details of this short trial. This time no witnesses were called because Jesus had already condemned himself by the claims that he had made. Caiaphas, along with others, once again cross-examined Jesus. 'Are you then the Son of God?' Jesus replied, 'You are right in saying I am.' This was all that was needed. Caiaphas then said to the court, 'Why do we need any more testimony? We have heard it from his own lips.'[23] This short trial was now at an end, and the death sentence had been ratified by the Sanhedrin, however illegally. The case was now remitted to Pilate who, as Roman Governor, had the power to carry out the death sentence.

Notes

1. *The Trial of Jesus Christ.*
2. John 18:13.
3. *Crucified and Crowned* (SCM Press).
4. John 18:20–22.
5. John 18:23, NEB.
6. John 18:24.
7. Mark 14:53, 55.
8. Acts 7.
9. John 8.
10. Matthew 26:59, 60.
11. Mark 14:56.

12. Matthew 26:61.
13. *The Real Jesus* (Hodder and Stoughton).
14. John 2:19, 21.
15. Mark 14:59.
16. Deuteronomy 19:18, 19.
17. Mark 14:60, 61.
18. Mark 14:61.
19. Mark 14:62.
20. *The Real Jesus* (Hodder and Stoughton).
21. Mark 14:64.
22. Mark 16:65.
23. Luke 22:70, 71.

6

Pontius Pilate

Who was the man who commanded the execution of Jesus? He has been described as the best known Roman of all time, more famous than Julius Caesar or Nero. Millions of Christians throughout the world remember him when every Sunday they recite the words of the Creed, 'I believe in Jesus Christ... who...suffered under Pontius Pilate.'

But until recently, apart from the reference to Pilate in the Gospels and the writings of the Jewish historian Josephus, there was no other evidence that Pilate ever existed. Then, during the summer of 1961, some Italian archaeologists were excavating an ancient theatre at Caesarea, the port in the Mediterranean that used to be the Roman capital of Palestine. As they worked they unearthed a large stone which had part of an inscription on it. When it was cleaned they were able to reconstruct the original inscription. There in three-inch lettering were the Latin words

CAESARIENS. TIBERIEVM
PONTIVS PILATVS
PRAEFECTUS IVDAEAE
DEDIT

'Pontius Pilate, Prefect of Judaea, has presented the
Tiberieum to the Caesareans.'

Much to their amazement the Italians had found
the first archaeological evidence for the existence of
Pontius Pilate. It is significant that he was described
as prefect of Judaea. As such he was not only a
Roman administrator but a governor with military
responsibility. What sort of a man was Pilate?
He became Governor of Palestine, with the Governor of Syria as his immediate superior, in around 26
AD. The previous Governor, Valerius Gratus, was
recalled to Rome because he had had trouble with
the Jews. Palestine was a frontier province of the
Roman Empire and already had the reputation of
being not an easy place to govern. Though we know
nothing about the career of Pilate before he came to
Palestine, he must have been a man of some ability
before he was posted by the Roman Emperor,
Tiberius, to such a difficult post in the Empire.
Sadly, from the beginning of his term of office, Pilate,
like his predecessor, was in trouble with the Jews.
Somehow he failed to understand them and was
lacking in diplomacy. Apart from the trial of Jesus,
we know of four other incidents in which Pilate and
the Jews were in conflict.

1. The affair of the Roman standards
As the occupying power the Romans respected the
religious views of the Jews, including their abhor-
rence of idols. God had said in the Ten Commandments 'You shall not make for yourself an idol in the
form of anything in heaven above or on the earth
beneath or in the waters below. You shall not bow

down to them or worship them.'[1] But at the time of Pilate's governorship, Emperor worship was beginning in the Roman Empire, and Roman soldiers were being encouraged not only to recognise the Emperor as king, but also to worship him as one of their gods. As a result they carried on their standards little images of the Emperor as a sign of his power. To the Jews these were graven images and so deeply offensive.

The Roman soldiers in Jerusalem were quartered in the Tower of Antonia, which overlooked the Jewish temple court. Up to the time of Pilate every Roman commander had marched his troops into Jerusalem without the image of the Emperor on their standards. But, soon after his arrival, Pilate sent a fresh garrison of troops to Jerusalem by night and ordered them to take with them their standards with the Emperor's image on them.

When the Jews woke up the next morning to find these standards under the shadow of the temple they were outraged. Immediately there was an uproar and many of them marched in protest from Jerusalem to the Roman headquarters at Caesarea. There they staged a five-day mass demonstration, protesting to Pilate about this gross violation of Jewish religious law. Instead of showing respect, Pilate was stubborn and would not yield to their request. He ordered his troops to surround the protestors and threatened them with instant death if they did not disband at once. But the Jews were made of sterner stuff and refused to go away. They bared their necks and challenged the Roman soldiers to cut their heads off. They would rather die than have these images in

Jerusalem. Pilate, who had obviously not expected this depth of feeling, could not risk a wholesale massacre. He then had to climb down and order the offensive standards to be removed. His first test of strength with the Jews had ended in a humiliating defeat. This did not augur well for the future.

2. The affair of the aqueduct

For a long time the water supply to Jerusalem had been inadequate and Pilate constructed a new aqueduct to improve the water supply. At first sight this should have been popular and a worthy cause. But Pilate financed the construction of the aqueduct with funds from the Jewish temple treasury. This enraged the Jews, who felt that their funds should not have been used for this purpose. While this action of Pilate must have been made with some co-operation from the priests in Jerusalem, riots soon broke out all over the city. Pilate acted quickly. He surrounded the rioters with Roman soldiers disguised as civilians. At a given signal they beat the mob with their staffs and, despite orders to the contrary, some of them drew their swords. As a result there was bloodshed and order was restored very soon. This time Pilate had won but the price was too high, and the relationship between him and the Jews had continued to worsen.

3. The affair of the wooden shields

On another occasion Pilate set up some wooden shields in the Roman headquarters in Jerusalem. Unlike the Roman standards they bore no image, but they were dedicated to the Emperor Tiberius. Again the Jews protested, seeing this as an affront to their religion. In their eyes it was a subtle attempt to introduce Emperor worship within the Holy City itself. Again they protested to Pilate but again he stubbornly refused to have the shields removed. The Jews then appealed to the Roman Emperor himself and wrote a letter of protest to him. In a strongly worded reply the Emperor wrote back, ordering Pilate to remove the shields and to transfer them at once to Caesarea. He also ordered Pilate to uphold the religious customs of the Jews. Thus Pilate had been soundly and humiliatingly defeated by the Jews. It was after this incident that he had to take the decisions about the trial of Jesus, and this helps to explain his conduct.

4. The last conflict

The last incident in Pilate's career involved the Samaritans, a tribe of people related to the Jews who still exist to this day, and were discriminated against by the Jews. A false prophet arose among them who promised that he would uncover the sacred vessels of the tabernacle. These, according to tradition, had been hidden by Moses in Mount Gerizim. This caused a sensation amongst the Samaritans and many of them assembled to go up this mountain together. Some of them arrived with weapons which alarmed the Roman authorities. Pilate ordered his troops to block all the roads leading to Mount Gerizim. A pitched battle then began and many of the Samaritans were killed. Also, some of their most influential leaders were executed on the spot. The Samaritan Senate protested to Pilate's immediate superior, the Governor of Syria, accusing him of murder and using excessive force. The Governor of

Syria ordered Pilate to return to Rome and to answer to the Emperor Tiberius the charges made against him. Pilate had no choice and, late in 36 AD, departed for Rome. But before he reached there the Emperor died. History does not record what subsequently happened. Was the judge, Pontius Pilate, himself judged in Rome? We simply do not know.

These four incidents give us a picture as to the sort of man Pilate was. He was a typical Roman of his day; arrogant and with little understanding of the Jews whose Governor he was. Above all, he was stubborn and unyielding. But when he came face to face with Jesus and had to judge him he became a different man. In many ways he seemed to be secretly admiring Jesus the accused, unsure of himself and strangely accommodating to the Jewish authorities. So what really happened in the Roman court that day? Whatever it was, it made Pilate not only the best known Roman, but also the best known judge who has ever lived.

Note

1. Exodus 20:4, 5.

7

The First Roman Trial

The Jewish trial of Jesus had been characterised by prejudice and hatred. The Romans, however, had no personal feelings against Jesus, and the justice given by Roman law was famous. We would expect Roman law to give Jesus a fair trial. But this was not to be the case; in fact things got worse. Frank Morison says:

> If anyone thinks that in approaching the trial of Jesus of Nazareth by Pontius Pilate he is approaching the simple and the obvious he is making a big miscalculation. This thing is very subtle. Outwardly it has all the placidity of still waters, but beneath the apparent stillness there are deep and hidden currents which make it incomparably the greatest and most profoundly interesting psychological study in history. We do not get rid of the mystery of Christ when we bring him to the Roman bar; we increase it tenfold.[1]

One of these mysteries is as to whether Pilate had come to some understanding with the Jewish authorities before Jesus appeared before him on trial. The account of the trial shows that this is more than likely. For a start, Pilate would not normally have held court on the eve of the Jewish Passover. But the Gospels record that as a concession to the Jewish authorities he did agree to try Jesus straight away. The Jews expected Pilate to simply ratify the death sentence already passed on Jesus, as the Passover approached. But much to their surprise he refused to do this. Then there is the urgent message sent by Pilate's wife to her husband while in court, 'Don't have anything to do with that innocent man.' It is difficult to explain this unless she had prior knowledge of the trial of Jesus. Such knowledge could only have come from her husband who in turn must have obtained it from the Jewish authorities.

The fullest description of this trial is found in John's Gospel, which was written primarily for Gentile believers. This account would be of great interest to his readers, many of whom would, like Jesus, be compelled one day to stand before a Roman court because of their faith. We know that John along with Peter managed to gain entrance into the court of the High Priest. John may then have followed Jesus as he entered the Praetorium, which was the official residence of Pilate. This would explain the detailed account which John gives us of this trial and his description of the dramatic moment in which Jesus confronts Pilate, his judge.

Roman courts began to sit shortly after daybreak. The Roman Seneca mentions 'Thousands hurrying to the forum at the break of day—how base their case is, and how much baser are their advocates'. Even in those days lawyers were not popular! Caiaphas probably remitted the case to Pilate around dawn, and the trial took place soon afterwards. John records that 'to avoid ceremonial uncleanness the Jews did not enter the palace; they wanted to be able to eat the Passover. So Pilate came out to them.'[2] Jewish law taught that the houses of the Gentiles were ceremonially unclean, and that any Jew who entered one of them would be also considered unclean for seven days afterwards, and would not be able to observe the Passover feast. It is a sad commentary to find that Caiaphas and the Jewish authorities were concerned about a ceremonial uncleanness that would prevent them from keeping the Passover, but they were not at all concerned about Jesus, who claimed to be the Messiah. Instead they planned to kill him.

This early morning trial of Jesus before Pilate was not a full trial according to Roman law. There was, in fact, no need for Pilate to follow Roman legal procedure at all, for Jesus was not a Roman citizen but merely a Jewish peasant to whom the laws of Rome did not apply. However, Pilate did follow Roman legal procedure to some extent. It seems that he was aware as he sat in court that Jesus was no ordinary man. Certainly, he realised that 'it was out of envy that they had handed Jesus over to him.'[3]

1. The charge

Roman law has had a great influence on English law, and Pilate's first question in this trial was the same one that any English lawyer would ask today: 'What have you been accused of?' When Caiaphas and the others brought Jesus to him 'Pilate came out to them and asked, "What charges are you bringing against this man?"'[4] Caiaphas appears to have been surprised at this. Evidently he thought that Pilate would simply ratify the death sentence and 'rubber stamp' the verdict of the Jewish court. But this was not to be. Taken aback and resenting Pilate's insistence on re-trying the case, the Jews curtly replied, 'If he were not a criminal we would not have handed him over to you.' Pilate then made his first attempt to get rid of the case. With ill-concealed impatience he retorted 'Take him yourselves and judge him by your own law.' But if Jesus were to be sentenced to death this was the one thing they could not do. They hastily replied, 'But we have no right to execute anyone.'

Pilate had still not had an answer to his question, and so Jesus had not been charged. Without a charge he could not be tried. The Jewish authorities were in a dilemma. They could not reveal the true nature of their charge, blasphemy. Pilate, as a Roman and pagan, would not be concerned about this. So they hastily re-framed their charge. Their determination to kill Jesus is seen in the way in which they did this. They now brought a charge against him which was not even mentioned in the Jewish trial and which was quite obviously false; 'We have found this man subverting our nation. He opposes payment of taxes to Caesar and claims to be Christ, a king.'[5] The first charge, that of 'subverting our nation', was very vague, and, unless some definite act could be proved, could be easily disproved. The second charge, 'He opposes payment of taxes to Caesar,' was obviously false. That very week, in answer to the trick question, 'Is it right for us to pay taxes to Caesar or not?', Jesus had given his famous reply, 'Give to Caesar what is Caesar's, and to God what is God's.'[6] But the last charge, 'He claims to be Christ, a king,' was a serious one. The Jewish authorities were accusing Jesus of being a revolutionary against Rome. Pilate must have been surprised to find the Jews, of all people, suddenly becoming champions of Rome. But this was a charge which he could not ignore. The authority of the Roman Emperor was at stake. The charge was treason.

2. The interrogation

The Roman statute on treason was the *Lex Julia Majestatis*, 48 BC. It made it an offence to engage in any activity against the Emperor or the Commonwealth. It could have been argued that Jesus was an alien and owed no duty to the Roman State, but as a Jew living in Roman-occupied territory he did owe allegiance to Caesar. When, in 6 AD, the Emperor agreed to make Palestine a Roman province, the Jewish nation gave their allegiance to Caesar. Any breach of this by a Jew was treason.

Now that the charge had been made, the next step was to examine the accused. To do this Pilate returned to the Praetorium, and took his seat upon the *bema*, a portable chair or throne, with Jesus in front of him.

In a scene full of dramatic power John pictures for us, the lowly majesty of Jesus confronting the proud majesty of Rome's representative. At this moment all the other actors in the passion recede from the attention. The basic thing is the confrontation of Caesar by Christ, with kingship as the topic for discussion.[7]

Pilate summoned Jesus and the accounts in all four Gospels record his first question, 'Are you the

70

king of the Jews?' The word 'you' is emphatic. As
Pilate looked at Jesus he was surprised that anyone
should be suggesting that he was a king. Certainly he
didn't look like one! Jesus replied, 'Is that your own
idea or did others talk to you about me?' This question makes a vital distinction. There were two ways
in which the word 'king' might be understood. It
could refer to a political king conspiring against Caesar—a resistance leader. If this was what Pilate
meant the answer was 'No'. But it could refer to a
messianic king of the Jews, in which case the answer
was 'Yes'. Pilate retorted, 'Am I a Jew? It was your
people and your chief priests who handed you over to
me. What is it you have done?' Pilate realised that
the accusation had come from the Jewish authorities.
He then asked Jesus what he had done to arouse
their hostility. He wanted to find out whether Jesus
had committed an offence against Roman law.

3. The defence

Jesus had now to answer the charge made against
him. Instead of pleading 'Not guilty' he made a plea
known in English law as 'Confession and Avoid-
ance'. This is a common defence.

> Jesus said in effect, 'In answer to the charge, I "confess
> and avoid"; that is to say, I admit I made and do make
> the claim alleged against me, I assert that that claim, in
> the sense in which I made it, is true in substance and in
> fact. I do not, however, make the claim in the sense
> alleged by my accusers. I admit that I claim to be a
> king, but not the sort of king alleged by the chief priests.
> I make no claim to be a king, a rival to Caesar. I am not
> guilty of treason against the Emperor. I admit and

assert that I have come to found a kingdom but not an earthly one; my kingdom is not of this world: If my kingdom were of this world, then would my servants fight, that I should not be delivered to the Jews: but now is my kingdom not from hence.'[8]

Pilate took the point and replied, 'You are a king, then!' Jesus answered, 'You are right in saying I am a king. In fact, for this reason I was born, and for this I came into the world, to testify to the truth. Everyone on the side of truth listens to me.'[9] Pilate must have been startled when he heard these words. Here was a king who was different. Jesus claimed to be king in a unique sense; king as no earthly ruler had ever been or could be. Pilate replied with his famous words, 'What is truth?' Francis Bacon suggests that Pilate was not serious when he asked this question; 'What is truth? said jesting Pilate, and would not stay for an answer.' But this could have been a serious question. Certainly, Pilate remembered Jesus' words. When the chief priests and the Jewish authorities protested about the notice over the cross of Jesus, 'This is the King of the Jews', he refused to change it. Whoever Jesus was it was clear that he was no rebel.

4. The acquittal

In Roman law three forms of verdict were possible; not guilty (*absolvo*), guilty (*condemno*) and doubtful (*non-liquest*). Scots law still has these three possible verdicts.

Pilate could have given in to the Jewish authorities and condemned Jesus to death because he was a revolutionary against Rome. But Pilate realised that

THE FIRST ROMAN TRIAL

this was not the case. Then he could have given a verdict of doubtful ('not proven'). This would have had the effect of referring the case back for a new trial on another day. There could have been justification for this because of the unsatisfactory nature of the evidence. But Pilate, whatever his other faults, acted with justice and gave a just sentence. Descending from his Judgement Seat and taking Jesus with him he went out to the chief priests and the crowd, who had been waiting impatiently, and gave his final decision, 'I find no basis for a charge against him.'[10] The trial was at an end and the prosecution had failed. The court ought to have then been cleared and the prisoner set free. But Pilate's words, far from ending the case, made matters worse and stirred up the crowd into a frenzy. They shouted out, 'He stirs up the people all over Judea by his teaching. He started in Galilee and has come all the way here.'[11]

When Pilate heard the word 'Galilee' he asked whether Jesus was a Galilean. He must immediately have realised that this was another opportunity of getting rid of the case. If Jesus belonged to Galilee, the man to handle his trial should be the local ruler of Galilee, Herod. Pilate, while he could have given Jesus a full trial himself, also had power after a preliminary examination to remit the case to Herod who was also in Jerusalem at that time. Not only did this get Pilate out of a painful dilemma, but it was a diplomatic master-stroke. Sometime previously, Pilate and Herod had quarrelled badly; this gesture on Pilate's part would help to heal the breach. Pilate hoped that not only would Herod now deal with this case but that he would be flattered as well.

The trial by Herod

So Jesus now went to be tried by Herod. This particular Herod—Herod Antipas—was the son of the
Herod who ordered the slaughter of the babies at
Bethlehem when Jesus was born. It was Herod
Antipas who had murdered John the Baptist at a
whim of his step-daughter and who was at this time
living with Herodias, the wife of his own brother
Philip. When he saw Jesus, he was delighted, for he
had been wanting to see him for a long time. When
Herod first heard of Jesus 'he was perplexed, for
some were saying that John [the Baptist] had been
raised from the dead, others that Elijah had appeared,
and still others that one of the prophets of long ago
had come back to life.'[12] Subsequently, Herod had
tried to kill Jesus, mainly because of his superstitious
fear that he was John the Baptist who had risen from
the dead. This was now his hour of opportunity. He
was hoping to see Jesus perform a miracle.

Herod tried to cross-examine Jesus as a lawyer
cross-examines a witness, but he was disappointed.
Jesus was not willing to satisfy his idle curiosity and
work a few miracles for the entertainment of him and
his friends. He answered none of the questions that
were put to him. Jesus was exercising an elementary
legal right when he remained silent. But his silence
meant more than this. It spoke more eloquently than
words. While Jesus had answers for his Jewish and
Roman judges he had no answer for this murderer
playing at holding a court of justice.

Nothing could have been more galling to Herod
than the silence with which his questions were
received. Herod was infuriated. He joined his sol-

diers in ridiculing and mocking Jesus. 'Dressing him in an elegant robe, they sent him back to Pilate. That day Herod and Pilate became friends—before this they had been enemies.'[13] Pilate had paid his respects to Herod and in turn Herod had paid his respects to Pilate by sending Jesus back. Behind all this was Herod's refusal to deal further with this case. Why did he miss this opportunity of giving Jesus a proper trial and passing a sentence of death upon him? Deep down Herod feared Jesus. His conscience still bothered him about his murder of John the Baptist. Also, while he was willing to join in mocking Jesus it was quite another thing to try him and sentence him to death. Herod knew that he had done nothing worthy of this. Once again the ball was back in Pilate's court.

Notes

1. *Who Moved the Stone?* (Faber & Faber/STL Books).
2. John 18:28, 29.
3. Matthew 27:18.
4. John 18:29.
5. Luke 23:2.
6. Matthew 22:21.
7. Leon Morris, *The Gospel According to John* (Marshall, Morgan and Scott).
8. Frank J. Powell, *The Trial of Jesus Christ* (Paternoster Press).
9. John 18:37.
10. John 18:38.
11. Luke 23:5.
12. Luke 9:7, 8.
13. Luke 23:11.

8

The Second Roman Trial

The return of Jesus to Pilate was a bitter, though not
unexpected, blow. Pilate thought he had got rid of
this case but, like a boomerang, it had come back to
him and now he had to take some action. The crowds
were getting out of control, and Pilate's authority as
Governor was seriously threatened. But he was still a
just man and for the second time he declared that
Jesus was innocent. 'You brought me this man as one
who was inciting the people to rebellion. I have
examined him in your presence and have found no
basis for your charges against him. Neither has
Herod, for he has sent him back to us; as you can see,
he has done nothing to deserve death. Therefore, I
will punish him and then release him.'[1] This punishment was flogging, and despite its illegality Pilate
hoped that this cruelty would satisfy the crowd. But
to them this was a sign that Pilate was weakening.
Far from being satisfied they demanded that Jesus be
crucified. In desperation Pilate decided to take
advantage of a Jewish custom by which the Roman
Governor in Passover week released a prisoner as a
gesture of good will. There is a precedent for this in

Roman law. 'An imperial magistrate could pardon and acquit individual prisoners in response to the shouts of the populace.'[2]

Among the prisoners held by the Romans at this time there was one, interestingly enough, also called Jesus—Jesus Barabbas. This man was a prisoner of some notoriety, a bandit and a murderer, and a member of a local resistance movement which to many of the Jews would make him a hero. The crowd was given a choice. Should Jesus Barabbas or Jesus Christ be released? Pilate expected the crowd to choose Jesus Christ. He also hoped to get himself out of his dilemma and to get the best of both worlds. If his plan succeeded Jesus would be released but, on the other hand, technically he would be convicted as a criminal who had then been acquitted.

While Pilate was sitting on his Judgement Seat waiting for the people to make their choice he received a message from his wife. She was Claudia Procula, the illegitimate daughter of Claudia, the third wife of the Emperor Tiberius. It has been suggested that it was due to her connections that Pilate had been appointed Prefect of Judaea. Her action was certainly unusual. Judges should not be interrupted when sitting in court. But Claudia had dreamt that night about Jesus. Perhaps she had heard him personally, and knew that her husband had made an arrangement with the Jewish authorities to try Jesus that day. This dream had impressed her and she sent the urgent message, 'Don't have anything to do with that innocent man, for I have suffered a great deal today in a dream because of him.'[3] The whole of human history would have changed if Pilate had paid attention to his wife's message. He did not, but this message strengthened his resolve to see that justice was done.

Pilate's plan to have Jesus released failed. While he waited in court for the crowd's decision the chief priests and the elders persuaded the crowd to choose Jesus Barabbas instead of Jesus Christ. They knew what this meant. Jesus Christ would be destroyed and sentenced to death. More desperate than ever, Pilate cried out, 'What shall I do, then, with Jesus who is called Christ?' The reaction was immediate and unanimous. Back came the reply, 'Crucify him!'[4]

It was now quite clear to Pilate that the chief priests and the crowd were determined to kill Jesus. As a last bid to satisfy them he made his final attempt to release Jesus. He carried out his earlier promise and took Jesus and had him flogged. Flogging was usually the preliminary to crucifixion. It was a terrifying punishment. The victim was stripped, tied to a pillar or stake and then beaten with a whip made up of leather lashes to which pieces of metal and bone were inserted. No maximum number of strokes was prescribed by law. Very often the victim's back was reduced to a pulp and many died beneath the lash before they came to the torment of crucifixion itself. But Pilate was still hoping to satisfy the crowd's blood-lust and make them willing to let Jesus go free. Lenski says, 'Jesus was not scourged in order to be crucified but in order to escape crucifixion.'[5]

While flogging Jesus, the Roman soldiers could not resist some crude horse-play. Jesus had been accused of being 'King of the Jews', so they would treat him as a king. They 'twisted together a crown of thorns and put it on his head. They clothed him in a purple robe and went up to him again and again, saying, "Hail, O king of the Jews!" And they struck him in the face.'[6] Jesus was then taken outside. The very sight of him should have been enough to show the crowd that he could not possibly claim to be a king, and thus allow Pilate to release him. But when Pilate said to the crowd, 'Here is the man!' it only stirred up the crowd to greater anger. Cries of 'Crucify! crucify!' now echoed through the court. Despite the fact that he had just had Jesus flogged, Pilate for the third time declared that he was innocent. 'I find no basis for a charge against him.' Pilate could have been talking to the wind for all the effect this had on the Jews. They insisted, 'We have a law, and according to that law he must die, because he claimed to be the Son of God.'

The truth was out. The real charge against Jesus was at last revealed. Pilate could not be called a religious man, but like many Romans of his day he was evidently superstitious. The Romans had many stories about gods appearing in human form. Pilate had been both intrigued and impressed by Jesus. Could there be something supernatural about him? He realised the seriousness of this charge and decided not to consider it publicly but to examine Jesus about it personally and in private. 'Where do you come from?' he asked Jesus. Could it be, he might have thought to himself, that the accused was indeed a man come from God? But Jesus did not answer. Previously he had answered other questions readily. Pilate persisted with his questioning. 'Don't you realise I have power either to free you or to crucify you?' Jesus answered, 'You would have no power over me if it were not given to you from above. Therefore the one who handed me over to you is guilty of a greater sin.' These were Jesus' last words to Pilate. He pointed out that the real responsibility for his trial rested with Caiaphas and the Jewish authorities. These words had a profound impact on Pilate. The truth was beginning to dawn. There was something different about this man—something God-like. The result was that 'from then on, Pilate tried to set Jesus free.' We do not know how Pilate tried to do this, 'but the Jews kept shouting, "If you let this man go, you are no friend of Caesar. Anyone who claims to be a king opposes Caesar." ' Later, they shouted, 'We have no king but Caesar.'[7] Again, this revealed the crowd's hostility towards Jesus. Caesar was certainly not their friend or their king. But they were determined that Jesus must be crucified.

The Jews' threat to report Pilate to Caesar amounted to blackmail. On a previous occasion the Jews had made a similar threat to send a deputation (or embassy) to Caesar. Philo tells us that Pilate 'feared that if they actually sent an embassy they would also expose the rest of his conduct as Governor by stating in full the briberies, the insults, the outrages and wanton injuries, the executions without trial constantly repeated, the ceaseless and supremely grievous cruelty.'[8] Pilate had already been in serious trouble with the Jews three times, and in no circumstances could he risk a complaint being lodged against him. He was outmanoeuvred and afraid of a riot; the Jews had got the better of him. 'Pilate yielded. He collapsed, miserably, utterly, and hurtled down the slippery slope of self-interest and expediency to his destruction. He abandoned his high duty as Judge to do right and justice to the accused without fear or favour, partiality, affection or ill-will; in an attempt to save himself from a charge of treason, he gave way to the clamour of the mob.'[9]

Pilate's last gesture was to wash his hands of the whole affair. He did this publicly, taking advantage of a Jewish custom. But he could not avoid the fact that the ultimate responsibility was his. Matthew records, 'Then he released Barabbas to them. But he had Jesus flogged, and handed him over to be crucified.'[10]

So the trial of Jesus was at an end. Pilate, the one man who could have obtained justice for Jesus, had handed him over to his executioners. And every time we say the Creed we remember that Jesus 'suffered under Pontius Pilate'.

Notes

1. Luke 23:14–16.
2. William L. Lane, *Gospel of Mark* (Eerdmans).
3. Matthew 27:19.
4. Matthew 27:22, 23.
5. *The Interpretation of St John's Gospel.*
6. John 19:2.
7. John 19:10–15.
8. Leg and Goé, 302.
9. Frank J. Powell, *The Trial of Jesus Christ* (Paternoster Press).
10. Matthew 27:26.

9

The Sentence

When Jesus was sentenced there was no doubt about what would happen. Under Jewish law the death sentence could be carried out by stoning, burning, beheading or strangling. Roman law added the torture of crucifixion. This was the most horrible of all punishments.

It had been invented by the Phoenicians. They had tried death by the spear, boiling in oil, stoning, strangulation, drowning and burning but all these had been found to be too quick. They wanted a way of punishing criminals slowly and inexorably, so they devised death by crucifixion. By it they could decide how much they wanted to hurt and how long it would take the victim to die. The victim's hands and feet were nailed to a cross. The victim might then hang there for two or three days until at last he suffocated or died either of exhaustion or starvation. From it we get our English word 'excruciating'.

It represented the acme of the torturer's art; atrocious physical sufferings, length of torment, ignominy, the effect on the crowd gathered to witness the long agony of the crucified. Nothing could be more horrible than the sight of this living body, breathing, seeing, hearing, still able to feel, and yet reduced to the state of a corpse by forced immobility and absolute helplessness. We cannot even say that the crucified person writhed in agony, for it was impossible for him to move. Stripped of his clothing, unable even to brush away the flies which fell upon his wounded flesh, already lacerated by the preliminary scourging, exposed to the insults and curses of people who can always find some sickening pleasure in the sight of the tortures of others, a feeling which is increased and not diminished by the sight of pain—the cross represented miserable humanity reduced to the last degree of impotence, suffering and degradation. The penalty of crucifixion combined all that the most ardent tormentor could desire: torture, the pillory, degradation, and certain death, distilled slowly drop by drop. It was an ideal form of torture.[1]

The Romans adopted crucifixion as a means of deterring crime. They reduced it to an exact science with a set of rules to be followed. On one occasion when they repressed a revolt we are told that six thousand men were crucified on a single day and hung on crosses between Capua and Rome. But no Roman citizen could be crucified; it was a punishment reserved for slaves and the worst type of criminals. Throughout the trial the Jews were determined that Jesus should be put to death and, eventually, through the weakness of Pilate, they had succeeded. The sentence was a foregone conclusion; death by crucifixion.

Note

1. A. Reville quoted by M. Goguel, *The Life of Jesus* (London).

10

A Lawyer's Viewpoint

Both historically and legally the trial of Jesus is unique. The theologian Professor S.G.F. Brandon of Manchester University comments,

> It would be difficult to resist its claim to be the most important trial in history, in view of the immensity and profundity of its consequences. If it were possible to assess the influence of Christianity on human culture and civilisation, that would be the measure of the historic importance of the trial of Jesus. Yet, when mentioned together with other historic trials, it is seen at once to be uniquely different. The trial of Jesus was an historical event, having occurred at a particular place and time, and involving other historical persons besides the chief character. But it is invested also with a religious significance, since the chief character has been regarded as a divine being, in fact as the Son of God.'[1]

Lawyers have also been fascinated by this trial. Amongst them are men far more eminent than I am. In the past Lord Shaw of Dunfermline, Lord of Appeal, described it as 'The greatest landmark in the history either of jurisprudence or of the world.' A famous Scots lawyer, A. Taylor Innes, writes 'The trial of Jesus is the most interesting isolated problem which historical jurisprudence can present.' More recently a Canadian judge, the Hon. James C. McRurer, Chief Justice of the High Court of Justice in Ontario, has written about the trial. He shows how it is all too easy for those in authority both in the time of Jesus and now 'to use the offices they hold to serve unworthy ends...sincerely believing that the end was a righteous one and the means justified.' Then in 1973 Israel's Supreme Court was petitioned to re-open the trial of Jesus. The application was submitted by a Jewish lawyer on behalf of David Biton of Eilat, in Israel. In his application, it was stated that Jesus was 'brought to trial because of hatred and because he was illegitimate and could not have had a fair trial. Since the Supreme Court judges are the heirs today of the Sanhedrin which tried Jesus...it is incumbent on them to undo the injustice done to Jesus.' The Court rejected the application. In its verdict it stated that it is accepted among historians that the Roman Commissioner, Pilate, not the Sanhedrin, judged Jesus. It queried whether a verdict attributing an injustice to the Sanhedrin would add respect to the Jewish nation of today. It also decided that the applicant had no personal interest in the case of Jesus which deals with a historic, not a legal, issue. In reporting this unique case the Jerusalem Post had the headline 'NO JUSTICE FOR JESUS'. The decision of the Israeli Supreme Court was obviously correct but that headline was still right. To me as a lawyer there are two things about this trial which stand out from the court record.

Justice was not done

According to the *Guinness Book of Records* the most successful criminal lawyer of all time is Sir Lionel Luckhoo of Guyana in the West Indies. By any standard he is a remarkable man. Not only has he been twice knighted for legal and diplomatic services by Queen Elizabeth but he was the first ambassador of his country to be accredited to Paris, Bonn and the Hague serving in the same capacities at the same time on behalf of a sister nation, Barbados. Legally his claim to fame is that he has defended in 245 murder trials and has obtained 245 acquittals! This is by far the longest run of successes in legal history. Not only is Sir Lionel an outstanding criminal lawyer but he is also a convinced Christian. Nowadays he spends much of his time speaking about his faith. As he does so he often speaks using legal knowledge 'to bring into focus the trial of Jesus before the Sanhedrin, Pilate and Herod, and to show how legal principles were twisted to crucify an innocent person.'[2]

With his record there is no doubt that if Sir Lionel had been alive at the time of Jesus he would have obtained his acquittal. I am certainly not even remotely as able a lawyer as he is but it is clear that there were many breaches of the law when Jesus was tried. I have already mentioned the difficulty there is in ascertaining exactly what the Jewish law was at the time of Jesus. But despite this, the law contained in the *Mishnah* does give us the Jewish ideal of justice, which the Sanhedrin should have followed. The discrepancies between how, according to the *Mishnah*, the Sanhedrin should have tried Jesus and how, according to the Gospels, they actually did so are so

THE TRIAL OF JESUS

great that some Jewish scholars maintain the
accounts in the Gospels are anti-Jewish inventions.
Haim H. Cohn, a Justice of the Supreme Court of
Israel, has gone so far as to suggest that the
Sanhedrin was seeking to find men to testify in
favour of Jesus and was attempting to persuade Jesus
to plead not guilty before the Romans. The latest
scholarship is against this. Also, every lawyer knows
of cases where there has been a miscarriage of justice.
But I have never heard of a lawyer who would then
argue from this that the court record must be wrong!

Let me detail some of the illegalities in the trial
before the Sanhedrin.

1. The Sanhedrin should not have plotted to kill
   Jesus. Its function was not only to protect but
   to be on the side of the accused.

2. It should not have looked for witnesses. In
   Jewish law it was the witnesses that com-
   menced proceedings.

3. It should not have looked for false witnesses.

4. The false witnesses should have been themselves punished.

5. Capital cases could not be tried at night.

6. Judgements in them had to be delayed until
   the next day.

7. Therefore capital cases could not be tried on
   the eve of a Sabbath or a festival day.

8. It was illegal to use the Oath of Testimony in
   a capital case.

9. Caiaphas should not have taken the case in his own hands and turned himself into Counsel for the Prosecution.

10. Capital cases had to open with arguments for acquittal.

11. Younger members were to speak first so as not to be influenced by the older members.

12. In capital cases all could not speak in favour of condemnation.

The very essence of justice is that the accused should have a fair trial. This was not the case here. After the witnesses disagreed, Jesus should have been freed, but Caiaphas and the Sanhedrin had made up their minds before the trial ever took place; whatever happened they were determined to secure a conviction. Justice was not done.

But the trial before Pilate and the Roman court was no better. It was far worse. At the end of the trial Pilate completely abrogated his responsibility as a judge. He should have declared that Jesus was innocent. Instead he sunk to the point where he asked the Jewish mob to decide about Jesus. I have never heard of a judge doing anything like this. Such conduct is unthinkable. Judges are appointed to try cases and not to ask others to do this for them!

Jesus was innocent

In the days when the death penalty was still in force there was much discussion as to whether an innocent person had ever been hanged. At that time a Member of Parliament wrote a book, *Hanged in Error*, dealing with six cases where, in his opinion, this had happened. This was one of the reasons why the death penalty was abolished. It is still a good reason why it should not be re-introduced. The latest attempt to do this in the British House of Commons was in June, 1988, when on a free vote a motion to restore the death penalty was defeated. The then British Home Secretary, Douglas Hurd, stated his personal opposition to the return of the death penalty because if capital punishment was introduced innocent people could be executed.

There is no doubt that this occasionally happened in the past. Above all, this was so with Jesus. It is remarkable to find that everyone who had anything to do with him said that he was innocent. His betrayer, Judas, before he went and hanged himself said 'I have betrayed innocent blood.'[3] Pilate's wife, in her urgent message to her husband while he was sitting in court, said, 'Don't have anything to do with that innocent man.'[4] The dying thief, the fellow victim of Jesus on the cross, said 'This man has done nothing wrong.'[5] Even his executioner, the Roman centurion, said, 'This was a righteous man.'[6] Above all, Pilate, the judge of Jesus, said three times 'I find no basis for a charge against him.'[7] But Pilate, through weakness and fear, allowed Jesus to be crucified. He did the worst thing any judge can do. To free a guilty man is one thing, but to condemn an innocent man to death is inexcusable. As has been pointed out by the Hon. James C. McRurer, 'In all the annals of legal history it would be difficult to find another case in which a prisoner who had been declared not guilty by a court of competent jurisdiction was delivered to the executioner by the judge who had acquitted him.'[8]

Frank J. Powell, a British barrister and Metropolitan magistrate with a lifetime's experience of London criminal courts concludes in his book on the trial: 'Both the Jewish and Roman courts professed to administer natural as well as legal justice. Neither did so in the case of Jesus; each court denied him both kinds of justice. Justice was not done and was manifestly and undoubtedly seen not to be done. JESUS OF NAZARETH, MESSIAH OF THE JEWS AND SAVIOUR OF THE WORLD, WAS MURDERED.'[9] That is dreadful enough. But is this all there is to the trial of Jesus? Is it nothing more than a unique legal case in which by a travesty of justice an innocent man was put to death?

Notes

1. *The Trial of Jesus of Nazareth* (Batsford).
2. Fred Archer, *Sir Lionel* (Gift Publications).
3. Matthew 27:4.
4. Matthew 27:19.
5. Luke 23:41.
6. Luke 23:47.
7. John 18:38; 19:4, 6.
8. *The Trial of Jesus* (Blandford Press).
9. *The Trial of Jesus* (Paternoster Press).

11

A Christian Viewpoint

To me as a Christian the trial of Jesus is much more than just a travesty of justice. It has not only a legal but also a far more important spiritual significance.

Man's sin

First, the trial shows us man's sin in all its stark nakedness. An American psychiatrist Karl Menninger has written a book called *Whatever Became of Sin?* That is a good question. Sin nowadays is not a popular subject. But though we don't like using the word, sin itself is still real. I have often asked myself the question, 'Who was responsible for crucifying Jesus?' Many wrong answers have been given. One answer is to say that Pontius Pilate and his soldiers were responsible. But the Gospels record that Pilate was pressurised into doing this by the Jewish authorities. So some people have claimed that the Jews, as a people, both then and now, are responsible for crucifying Jesus. Not only did medieval Christianity err in teaching this, but sadly there is still anti-Semitism today. The former teenage pop star, Helen

Shapiro, tells how she first heard the name of Jesus at the age of six. A child at school about her own age ran up to her in the playground one day screaming, 'You killed Jesus Christ!' This upset her deeply because she didn't even know who Jesus was and yet she had been accused of killing him.

Every true Christian must utterly repudiate this. It is ludicrous to draw the conclusion that, because a comparatively small number of Jewish priests crucified Jesus, all Jews since then are guilty of the same sin. Any idea of collective guilt is both legally and morally utterly wrong.

This slander on the Jewish nation was repudiated by the Second Vatican Council which clearly stated, 'While it is true that the Jewish authorities and those who followed their lead pressed for the death of Christ[1] nevertheless what happened in his passion cannot be charged against all the Jews, without distinction, then alive, nor against the Jews of today.'[2] All Christians must agree with this. Anti-Semitism is not only inexcusable but a denial of the Christian faith. Professor Paul L. Maier, Professor of Ancient History at Western Michigan University in America, well summarises this question of Jewish responsibility. 'To be anti-Semitic because of Good Friday would be as ridiculous as hating Italians because Nero once threw Christians to the lions.'[3]

Maybe instead of accusing others of crucifying Jesus, we should instead think of our own sins by which we are all guilty of his death. The Roman Catechism teaches that no single person but all men are guilty of Jesus' death. 'This guilt seems more enormous in us than in the Jews, since according to the testimony of the apostle [Paul], "Had they known it, they would never have crucified the Lord of Glory;"[4] while we, on the contrary, professing to know him, yet denying him by our actions, seem in some sort to lay violent hands on him.'[5] The Catechism is right. It is one thing to see the sins of others but another thing to see our own sins. What can we learn from the men who crucified Jesus?

Judas

What was wrong with Judas? Why did he betray Jesus for thirty pieces of silver? The tendency nowadays is to excuse Judas; to whitewash his character. It has been suggested that he was an honest patriot who had come to the conclusion that Jesus was a danger to the Jewish nation. Jesus was betrayed in order to save the nation and avoid a head-on clash with Rome. An opposite idea is that Judas wanted to force Jesus' hand and to compel him to act against the Romans. In this way Jesus would be made to exercise his power. His arrest would facilitate this. Yet another suggestion is that Judas was testing Jesus. He was not sure as to whether he was the Messiah. If Jesus was arrested, then this would be resolved. If he were the Messiah he would rescue himself; if he were not then he was an imposter and deserved to die.

Ingenious as these explanations are none of them are backed up by the Gospel accounts. I have often wondered why there is this modern tendency to excuse Judas. One answer could be that we are too like Judas ourselves but don't want to admit it. The plain fact of the matter is that Judas betrayed Jesus for money. John records, 'He was a thief; as keeper of the money bag, he used to help himself to what was put into it.'[6] Judas objected when Mary anointed Jesus' feet with expensive perfume. To him that was a waste of money. This fits in perfectly with his action in taking the bribe of thirty pieces of silver to betray Jesus.

The motive behind everything that Judas did was greed. He is a perfect illustration of the truth of Paul's words 'The love of money is a root of all kinds of evil. Some people, eager for money, have wandered from the faith and pierced themselves with many griefs.'[7] People will do anything to get money. This is true not only of the petty criminal but also of the successful businessman. It always amazes me how even those that are comparatively well-off still have this greed to get more. The old saying 'Money is like sea-water; the more a man drinks, the more thirsty he becomes' is all too true. In today's world of the so-called 'yuppies', materialism has become respectable. No longer is it regarded as a sin. We are not even conscious of it. The famous Roman Catholic, Francis Xavier, said that as a priest he had heard men confess all kinds of sins but never had anyone of their own free will confessed to being covetous. But greed and the love of money is a deadly sin. It was so in the case of Judas. We are no different. Through the years I have seen many reject Jesus Christ and his claims on their lives because, like the rich young ruler, they had great possessions. The fatal thing is that it was not they that had the possessions, but it was the possessions that had them. Judas is a warning to our modern materialistic world.

The soldiers

What about the Roman soldiers who crucified Jesus? Why did they do this? It could be argued that like soldiers the world over they were simply obeying orders. It was not theirs to reason why. But it is clear that these soldiers recognised that there was something different about Jesus. As he died the Roman centurion 'Seeing what had happened, praised God and said, "Surely this was a righteous man." '[8] But neither he nor any of the soldiers did anything to rescue Jesus. Instead we read that when they crucified him they gambled for his garments. 'And sitting down they watched him there.'[9]

The great sin of the soldiers was indifference. That is still true today. We are indifferent to each other. 'The worst sin towards our fellow creatures is not to hate them, but to be indifferent to them: that's the essence of inhumanity.'[10] But a greater sin is indifference towards Jesus Christ. That is the attitude of most people. It never ceases to amaze me that the clients who come to me as a lawyer have time for business, pleasure, everything under the sun but Jesus. Ultimately this is what separates us from God for ever. Contrary to what many think we do not have to commit a spectacular sin to be lost. We are lost already. The Bible warns 'How shall we escape if we ignore such a great salvation?'[11]

This attitude to Jesus is summed up in the well-known poem of Studdert Kennedy. During the First

World War he was nicknamed 'Woodbine Willie'
because of his habit of going to the men at the front
giving out Woodbine cigarettes and New Testa-
ments. As he spoke about his faith in this way he
found a ready response. But after the war, when
Studdert Kennedy spoke to businessmen, things
were different. Their self-sufficiency was hard to
bear. His poem 'Indifference' sums it up:

When Jesus came to Golgotha they hanged him on a
    tree,
They drove great nails through hands and feet, and
    made a Calvary;
They crowned him with a crown of thorns, red were his
    wounds and deep,
For those were crude and cruel days, and human flesh
    was cheap.

When Jesus came to Birmingham they simply passed
    him by,
They never hurt a hair of him, they only let him die;
For men had grown more tender, and they would not
    give him pain,
They only just passed down the street, and left him in
    the rain.

Still Jesus cried, 'Forgive them, for they know not what
    they do,'
And still it rained the wintry rain that drenched him
    through and through;
The crowds went home and left the streets without a
    soul to see,
And Jesus crouched against a wall and cried for Calv-
    ary.

Herod

What about King Herod? When Jesus was on trial before him why didn't he set him free? Instead he lost his temper and joined his soldiers in mocking Jesus before sending him back to Pilate. The answer is simple. Herod was guilty of lust. He was living with Herodias, the wife of his brother Philip. When John the Baptist warned Herod 'It is not lawful for you to have her' he was imprisoned and then murdered. Herod was afraid of Jesus and of the truth about himself. He even wondered whether Jesus was John the Baptist risen from the dead.

Things have not changed. Ever since Sigmund Freud shocked the Victorian world by stating that all of life is permeated with a craving for sexual gratification there has been an obsession with sex.

As a lawyer I have seen an incredible increase in the divorce rate so that nowadays in England one marriage in every three ends in divorce. Adultery is the main cause of this. This obsession with sex keeps many from becoming Christians. Instead of their mastering sex it has mastered them. In fact the Bible's teaching about sex is very reasonable. Many have wrong ideas about it. As C.S. Lewis has said 'Chastity is the most unpopular of the Christian virtues.' Yet it should not be. God made sex for our benefit. It is good and should be rightly used in marriage. Contrary to popular belief it is the Christian who enjoys sex in all its fullness.

My experience over many years is that many reject Christianity not for intellectual but for moral reasons. Often, when I have presented the evidence for the Christian faith and the resurrection, people have admitted to me that they have been convinced that Jesus rose from the dead. But when asked 'Are you now going to become a Christian?' they have replied somewhat sheepishly 'No' and then added, 'Frankly it would mean too much of a change in my life-style.' And then in a moment of total honesty they would admit to me that this would be in the area of sex. Like Herod their lust stops them from coming to Jesus.

Caiaphas

What was wrong with Caiaphas, the High Priest? We have already seen that he was the real power behind the trial and the death of Jesus. What was his motive in all this? To me it is all too obvious. He was frightened that Jesus would be a rival ruler and interfere with the power held by himself and his family. His words 'It is better for you that one man die for the people than that the whole nation perish'[12] sum up his attitude to Jesus. He wanted to hold on to his power. His subsequent conduct is a perfect illustration of the truth of the well-known saying of Lord Acton, 'Power always corrupts and absolute power corrupts absolutely.'

Caiaphas put self-interest before Jesus. He is not the first or the last person to have done this. For years I have seen businessmen and fellow lawyers seeking after prestige and power. Behind it all is self and pride. Basically all sin is selfishness in some form or another but pride is the ultimate, 'the worship of self'. C.S. Lewis writes,

There is one vice of which no man in the world is free; which every one in the world loathes when he sees it in someone else; and of which hardly any people, except Christians, ever imagine that they are guilty themselves. I have heard people admit that they are bad-tempered, or that they cannot keep their heads about girls or drink, or even that they are cowards. I do not think I have ever heard anyone who was not a Christian accuse himself of this vice. And at the same time I have very seldom met anyone, who was not a Christian, who showed the slightest mercy to it in others. There is no fault which makes a man more unpopular, and no fault which we are more unconscious of in ourselves. And the more we have it ourselves, the more we dislike it in others. The vice I am talking of is Pride or Self-Conceit...pride leads to every other vice: It is the complete anti-God state of mind.

Pride takes many forms. There is intellectual pride leading to self-confidence instead of God-confidence. There is social pride which makes us consider ourselves better than others. But the most fatal of all is spiritual pride which stops us from seeing our own need. Not only did this lead to the death of Jesus but it still stops many from coming to faith. John Stott tells how when he was over in America taking a university mission a student asked him the question, 'Tell me in one sentence what Christianity is all about.' He replied, 'Jesus Christ wants to come into the centre of your life and you have to move over to the circumference.' To which the student with commendable honesty answered, 'Gee, I sure don't like the idea of de-centralisation!'

The chief priests

What about the chief priests? They plotted to kill Jesus. What was their motive? Mark in his Gospel gives the answer. He tells us that during the trial Pilate realised that 'It was out of envy that the chief priests had handed Jesus over to him.'[13] Most of us would not think of envy as being a great sin but the envy of the chief priests led to the death of Jesus. Pope Gregory the Great, at the end of the sixth century, divided all sins into seven categories and envy was one of them. Chrysostom, one of the early Church fathers, said, 'As a moth gnaws a garment so does envy consume a man.' How right he was!

Sadly religious people are particularly prone to envy. That was so with the chief priests. They were sincere religious men but jealous of Jesus and his popularity. They were not the first to be envious. The Bible has many examples of this and its dire consequences. Cain killed his brother Abel because he was envious that God had accepted his offering and not his own. Joseph's brothers were envious of him and sold him to the Egyptians. Saul tried to kill David because he envied his popularity.

Envy is still with us today. It is seen in the way in which we love to slander others, who we may see as more privileged than ourselves, and drag them down to our own level. Then in turn we like to be envied ourselves. One American economist claims that our spending habits are influenced by the enjoyment we get from others envying us and longing to possess the things we have. But ultimately, as in the case of the chief priests, envy kills.

There is a Greek story about a man who killed

himself through envy. His fellow citizens had erected a statue to one of their number who was a celebrated champion in the public games. But this man, a rival of the honoured athlete, was so envious that he vowed he would destroy that statue. Every night he went out into the darkness and chiselled at its base in an effort to undermine its foundation and make it fall. At last he succeeded. It did fall—but it fell on him. He fell, a victim of his own envy.[14]

Pilate

What was wrong with Pilate? He knew that Jesus was innocent but through weakness he allowed him to be crucified. The answer is fear. At heart he was a coward and afraid of others. This comes out time and time again in the account of the trial. Pilate was afraid of the crowds as they cried out for Jesus to be crucified, afraid that if he let Jesus go free he would be reported to Caesar and lose his post. The Bible warns us 'Fear of man will prove to be a snare.'[15] This was certainly true of Pilate. He was afraid of the consequences of his own actions. Behind this was a basic uncertainty. The man who is absolutely certain is impervious to fear.

I can identify with Pilate. Before I became a Christian I was an atheist. But as I examined the evidence I became convinced of the truth of Christianity. This did not mean that I was willing to become a Christian; I was afraid of what others would think. At heart fear stopped me from following Jesus. I am no exception. Through the years I have found that the same thing holds others back from becoming Christians. Christians are often ridiculed as being weak people but the truth is the exact opposite. The pressure of our non-Christian peer group is very strong. It takes courage to be a Christian. It is all too easy to be like Pilate. We need to be delivered from the fear of others.

It is not difficult to see the sins which made these men crucify Christ. It is not so easy to recognise them in ourselves. Contrary to what some people think this is not something which just involves them; it involves all of us. These same sins of greed, indifference, lust, pride and fear, which made these men crucify Jesus, are in our own lives. These sins stop us from becoming Christians. Because of them we reject Jesus and his claim to our lives. This is just as bad as physically crucifying him.

One man that recognised this was the Scots minister, Tom Allan, of Glasgow. He tells how one Easter Sunday morning towards the end of the war he went to church in Rheims in France.

The congregation was composed entirely of American servicemen. It was an American chaplain who took the service. I don't remember anything at all of what he said. But at one point in the service a G.I., a negro in the choir loft, got up and sang the spiritual, 'Were you there when they crucified my Lord?'

Now I had heard that sung hundreds of times. Indeed I'd sung it myself. But on that day in Rheims, as the negro soldier was singing, I realised for the first time—really for the first time—not as a theory, but on the pulses of my life, what the cross was about and what the Christian faith was about.

I realised for the first time that day that Christ had died for me. 'Were you there...?' How could I be there? This happened two thousand years ago. But the negro who first sang that spiritual had gone right to the heart of Christian truth and had in this simple spiritual, reminded us of the fact that we're all involved in the death of Christ. And I remember thinking that, if my hand had helped to crucify him, then also I was there when he prayed 'Father, forgive them.' I was involved in Calvary and I was involved also in the forgiveness of Cod through Christ. That day, I heard unmistakably speaking to me the voice of God.

Notes

1. John 19:6.
2. *Nostra Aetate*.
3. *First Easter* (Harper and Row).
4. 1 Corinthians 2:8.
5. *The Roman Catechism of Trent*.
6. John 12:6.
7. 1 Timothy 6:10.
8. Luke 23:47.
9. Matthew 27:36 (AV).
10. G.B. Shaw, *The Devil's Disciple*.
11. Hebrews 2:3.
12. John 11:50.
13. Mark 15:10.
14. Billy Graham, *The Seven Deadly Sins* (Marshall, Morgan and Scott).
15. Proverbs 29:5.

12

God's Love

The trial of Jesus also shows us the love of God. Many times I have asked myself the question 'Why did Jesus never attempt to defend himself?' As a lawyer I know that he had a perfect defence. He was innocent. But as a Christian I realise that there is something deeper here. We find Jesus telling us why he came into this world. He says, 'The Son of Man did not come to be served, but to serve, and to give his life as a ransom for many.'[1] In other words, all of us are born to live but Jesus said that he was born to die. His death on the cross was of his own free will. It was his deliberate choice, not his inevitable fate. This was no act of martyrdom, it was what Jesus came to do. 'I lay down my life—only to take it up again. No-one takes it from me, but I lay it down of my own accord.'[2]

There was never a time in the life of Jesus when he was not aware that the cross was his final destiny. John Stott in his book *The Cross of Christ*[3] quotes Octavius Winslow, 'Who delivered up Jesus to die? Not Judas, for money; Pilate, for fear; not the Jews, for envy;—but the Father, for love!' He then goes on to say, 'On the human level, Judas gave him up to the priests, who gave him up to Pilate, who gave him up to the soldiers, who crucified him. But on the divine level, the Father gave him up, and he gave himself up, to die for us. As we face the cross, then, we can say to ourselves both "I did it, my sins sent him there" and "He did it, his love took him there." ' What does the Bible tell us about this love of God which lies behind the cross?

The greatest love

First of all, the Bible tells us that God's love is great. 'For God so loved the world that he gave his one and only Son, that whoever believes in him shall not perish but have eternal life',[4] has been described as the greatest sentence ever written. It is the mini-gospel.

Many people have wrong ideas about God. It is not that he loves us because Christ died for us, but that Christ died for us because God loves us. This is the greatest thing in all the world.

Payment for sin

God's love deals with our sins. When Jesus suffered and died on the cross he did so not only because of our sins but also for our sins. The Bible puts it very simply, 'Christ died for our sins.'[5] The word in the Greek translated 'for' is *huper*. This word does not mean 'because of' or 'in place of', but 'on behalf of' or 'for the sake of'. When Jesus died on the cross it was on our behalf. The punishment for our sins was taken by him. John Oxenham in one of his books imagines how Jesus Barabbas felt after he had been set free. He was fascinated by Jesus Christ and followed him to Calvary to see the end. As he saw Jesus hanging upon his cross he realised with awe, 'I should have been hanging there—not he—he has died in my place and saved me!' That is the heart of the cross.

> He died that we might be forgiven
> He died to make us good
> That we might go at last to heaven
> Saved by his precious blood.

A well known sketch 'God Leads a Pretty Sheltered Life' sums up how God in Christ bore our sins:

At the end of time, billions of people were scattered on a great plain before God's throne. Some of the groups near the front talked heatedly—not with cringing shame, but with belligerence.

'How can God judge us? How can he know about suffering?', snapped a joking brunette. She jerked back a sleeve to reveal a tattooed number from a Nazi concentration camp. 'We endured terror, beatings, torture, death!'

In another group, a black man lowered his collar. 'What about this?' he demanded, showing an ugly rope burn. 'Lynched for no crime but being black! We have suffocated in slave ships, been wrenched from loved ones, toiled till only death gave release.'

Far out across the plain were hundreds of such groups. Each had a complaint against God for the evil and suffering he permitted in his world. How lucky God was to live in heaven where all was sweetness and light, where there was no weeping, no fear, no hunger, no hatred! Indeed, what did God know about what man had been forced to endure in this world? 'After all, God leads a pretty sheltered life,' they said.

So each group sent out a leader, chosen because he had suffered the most. There was a Jew, a black, an untouchable from India, an illegitimate, a person from Hiroshima, and one from a Siberian slave camp. In the centre of the plain they consulted with each other. At last they were ready to present their case. It was rather simple: before God would be qualified to be their judge, he must endure what they had endured. Their decision was that God 'should be sentenced to live on earth—as a man!'

But, because he was God, they set certain safeguards to be sure he could not use his divine powers to help himself:

Let him be born a Jew.

Let the legitimacy of his birth be doubted, so that none will know who is really his father.

Let him champion a cause so just, but so radical that it brings down upon him the hate, condemnation, and eliminating efforts of every major traditional and established religious authority.

Let him try to describe what no man has ever seen, tasted, heard, or smelled...let him try to communicate God to men.

Let him be betrayed by his dearest friends.

Let him be indicted on false charges, tried before a prejudiced jury, and convicted by a cowardly judge.

Let him see what it is to be terribly alone and completely abandoned by every living thing.

Let him be tortured and let him die!

Let him die the most humiliating death with common thieves.

As each leader announced his portion of the sentence,

loud murmurs of approval went up from the great throng of people. When the last had finished pronouncing sentence, there was a long silence. No one uttered another word. No one moved. For suddenly all knew...God had already served his sentence.

No strings attached

God's love is undeserved. Masumi Toyotome has pointed out that there are three kinds of love. The first is the 'if' kind of love. This is the lowest form; it is conditional. The love which will be given to us 'if' we meet certain requirements. This kind of love is all too common. It is love with strings attached. We say to our children, 'If you are good, father will love you.' Men say to their sweethearts, 'If you promise to marry me, I will give you my love.' Worse still we can even say to God, 'If you bless me, I will love you.' Basically this love is selfish. It appeals to the lowest in us. We want to gain something before we give our love. This love doesn't last. When we cease to get what we want we cease loving. This kind of love may be behind the alarming increase in the divorce rate. When we don't get what we want we stop loving.

The second kind of love is the 'because' kind of love. Here we love someone because of what they have or what they can do for us; 'I love you because you are so beautiful,' 'I love you because you are so good to me,' or 'I love you because you are so right, or famous.' Whilst this kind of love is better than the 'if' kind of love it is still far from satisfactory. At first we may be flattered. I am loved because I am good-looking or wealthy. But what happens if I cease to be

109

like this? This kind of love leads to insecurity and fear.

In his booklet on the three kinds of love Masumi Toyotome recounts the tragic story of a beautiful young woman in Japan who was working in a cleaning establishment. One day a boiler exploded and the fluid burnt her face, chest and hands. Her features were so badly disfigured that in the hospital she always wore a bandage over her whole face and allowed no one to see her except her doctor. The young man to whom she was engaged broke off their engagement. During the few months she was in the hospital until her death, her parents, although living in the same city, did not come to see her. The love she enjoyed disappeared overnight. It was based on her loveliness. With it gone, the love was gone.

The third kind of love is the 'in spite of' love. It has no strings attached. It does not depend on anything we have or do. We are loved 'in spite of' all these things. This is the greatest kind of love, the love which all of us long for. What a relief it is not to have to bargain for love but just to know that we are loved despite all that we are! The supreme example of this kind of love is when Jesus died on the cross. 'God demonstrates his own love for us in this: While we were still sinners, Christ died for us.'[6] As Jesus died he loved even those who were crucifying him and prayed, 'Father, forgive them, for they do not know what they are doing.'[7] This is 'in spite of' love indeed. When man was doing his worst, the love of Jesus was at its best. This love was not just for then but for all time. God loves us exactly as we are, in spite of all that we have done. None of us deserve it, but this love is ours.

Love for all

Finally, the greatest thing of all is that God loves each of us despite who we are or what we have done. As I was writing this chapter I had the unique experience of taking part in a Christian mission to Strangeways Prison in Manchester. After the showing of a video of a Billy Graham meeting I counselled a man who was deeply distressed. With tears in his eyes he confessed that he was in jail for murdering his mother. He felt that his sin was so great that God could not possibly love him or forgive him. It was my privilege to share with him the good news that God really loves us. The great proof of this is the death of Jesus on the cross; 'This is how we know what love is: Jesus Christ laid down his life for us.'[8] This was good news indeed to that prisoner and it is good news for every one of us.

Several years before his death Dr Karl Barth, the great Swiss theologian—probably the greatest theologian of his day—was visiting America. After a lecture at a seminary a student asked him the question, 'Dr Barth, what is the greatest thought that has ever passed through your mind?' For a moment it seemed that Dr Barth was stumped. He bowed his head and paused for a long time. Then he slowly lifted his head and everyone thought some tremendous statement was coming forth. They were all on the edge of their seats when he said with great simplicity:

Jesus loves me! This I know,
For the Bible tells me so.

That is very simple but utterly profound. God loves each one of us as if there were no one else to love. This is the greatest thing in all the world. But is that the end? William Morris wrote a poem entitled 'Love is Enough.' Someone reviewed it by saying simply, 'It isn't!' Love demands a response.

Notes

1. Mark 10:45.
2. John 10:17,18.
3. Inter-Varsity Press.
4. John 3:16.
5. 1 Corinthians 15:3.
6. Romans 5:8.
7. Luke 23:34.
8. 1 John 3:16.

Conclusion: Our Verdict

When Pilate met Jesus he was faced with the greatest decision of his life. His question, 'What shall I do, then, with Jesus who is called Christ?',[1] has been described as the most important question that any man ever asked or answered.

First, Pilate's question is important because much depended upon it. The fate of Jesus depended upon it. The reputation of Roman justice was bound up with it. All these things Pilate must have been aware of, but there was something else beyond this. What he did not realise that day was that his own place in history and his own fate was bound up with what he did with Jesus.

This is the case not only with Pilate but with us. Our finding peace of mind depends on what we do with Jesus. We can fill our lives with a hundred interests and activities. But if we leave Jesus out of our lives we will never have perfect peace of mind. As Augustine prayed years ago, 'Lord, you have made us for yourself and our hearts are restless until they find their rest in you.' Our finding real joy depends on what we do with Jesus. Everyone wants to be happy, but so often this eludes us. Jesus came to give us life in all its fullness. But, above all, our eternal destiny depends on what we do with Jesus.

As a lawyer I must have made thousands of wills for my clients. Some years ago I wrote a short leaflet *Now that You Have Made Your Will*, giving advice about keeping one's will safe and reviewing it from time to time. I ended with a final word:

> Your will is not only the most important legal document that you will ever make, but it also inevitably brings before all of us the fact of death. It is amazing how many people delay making a will just because they are reluctant to face death. It is the last thing we want to talk about. However, I am convinced that death is not the end. I trust you will not think it presumptuous for me to suggest that you should have a word either with a Christian minister or myself about this. After all, what is going to happen to you in the future is far more important than what is going to happen to your estate.

The real significance of this trial is that looked at in the blazing light of eternity, Jesus was not judged but in fact he was the judge. The Bible teaches, 'He is the one whom God appointed as judge of the living and the dead.'[2] On the day of final judgement it is our relationship to Jesus which will count. Our eternal destiny will depend upon it. Nothing is more important than this.

Secondly, Pilate's question about Jesus is vitally important because it concerns such a vitally important person. Pilate had to make up his mind about Jesus. Who was this man? Was he just a troublesome

Galilean peasant or was he what he claimed to be—
a king?

Who is Jesus?

Throughout his life Jesus made incredible claims
about himself. He claimed to be eternal. When asked
about himself he said, ' "I tell you the truth...before
Abraham was born, I am!" At this, [the Jews] picked
up stones to stone him.'[3] Others are born to live but
Jesus claimed that he lived before he was born! This
amounted to blasphemy and the penalty for this was
stoning.

Then Jesus claimed to be sinless. Negatively,
before his death he said to his disciples, 'I will not
speak with you much longer, for the prince of this
world is coming. He has no hold on me.'[4] By saying
this Jesus was claiming that he had never done anything wrong. Positively, on another occasion he said,
'I always do what pleases [my Father].'[5] This time
Jesus claims that he always did what is right. These
claims astonish us. Normally, the more holy a man is
the more he is aware of his own sin. Here we have the
paradox of a holy man declaring his own holiness.

But the greatest claim of all is the claim of Jesus to
be God. It was this claim that led to his death. At the
beginning of his ministry, 'The Jews tried all the
harder to kill him; not only was he breaking the
Sabbath, but he was even calling God his own
Father, making himself equal with God.'[6] Then later
on we read, 'The Jews picked up stones to stone him,
but Jesus said to them, "I have shown you many
great miracles from the Father. For which of these do

115

you stone me?" "We are not stoning you for any of these," replied the Jews, "but for blasphemy, because you, a mere man, claim to be God." [7] The culmination of the claim to be God was at the trial before the Sanhedrin. When Jesus said that he was the Messiah, the Son of God, the High Priest tore his garments and Jesus was condemned to death for blasphemy. By making this claim the trial of Jesus became unique in legal history. The question before the court was not the actions of Jesus but his identity; his claim to be God.

These claims force us to make up our minds about Jesus. No other religious leader has ever made anything like them. They were either true or false. If they are false we are faced with two alternatives.

Was he a liar?

The first alternative is that Jesus knew that his claims were false. If this is so, it means that he was not only a liar but the greatest deceiver of all time. It is hard to believe this. The whole character of Jesus is against it. Even non-Christians have paid tribute to his life and teaching. In the past the French unbeliever Rousseau said, 'If the life and death of Socrates are those of a philosopher, the life and death of Jesus Christ are those of a God.' In our day the pop star Mick Jagger has said 'Jesus Christ is fantastic and something to base life on.'

Was he a madman?

The second alternative is that Jesus did not know that his claims were false. If this is so it means that he was not only deluded but, because of the fundamental nature of his claims, mentally unbalanced— a lunatic. George Bernard Shaw, to whom nothing was sacred, described Jesus as 'a man who was sane until Peter hailed him as the Christ and who then became a monomaniac...His delusion is a very common delusion among the insane.'[8] But is this so? The teaching and life of Jesus are against it. He didn't speak or act like a madman. C.S. Lewis comments, 'The discrepancy between the depth and sanity and (let me add) shrewdness of his moral teaching and the rampant megalomania which must lie behind his theological teaching unless he is indeed God, has never been satisfactorily explained.'[9]

Is he God?

Once we have ruled out the possibility that the claims of Jesus were false, inexorably we are left with the conclusion that they are true. This man is what he claimed to be; namely eternal, sinless and even God himself. I find that most people will not face up to the logic of this. In a recent student survey seventy per cent of the men and eighty-five per cent of the women said that Jesus was a good, wise and great teacher. But logically he could not have been just this. He must have been infinitely more or infinitely less. If Jesus was not God he was not good because no good person would deliberately lie and mislead people as he did. No one has summed it up better than C.S. Lewis:

> I am trying to prevent anyone saying the really foolish thing that people often say about Jesus. 'I'm ready to accept him as a great moral teacher but I don't accept his claim to be God.' That is the one thing we must not say. A man who was merely a man and said the sort of things Jesus said would not be a great moral teacher. He would either be a lunatic—on a level with the man who says he is a poached egg—or else he would be the Devil of hell. You must make your choice. Either this man was, and is, the Son of God: or else a madman or something worse. You can shut him up for a fool, you can spit at him and kill him as a demon or you can fall at his feet and call him Lord and God. But let us not come with any patronising nonsense about his being a great human teacher. He has not left that open to us. He did not intend to.[10]

Your response

Above all, Pilate's question, 'What shall I do with Jesus?', is important because it cannot be evaded. We have already seen how Pilate tried to avoid making a decision about Jesus. He did this four times. When Jesus was first brought to him by the Jews he said to them, 'Take him yourselves and judge him by your own law,' but they replied, 'We have no right to execute anyone.' Then when Pilate heard that Jesus was a Galilean, like a drowning man clutching at a straw, he sent him to Herod, the ruler of Galilee. But Herod in turn sent Jesus back to Pilate. Pilate then remembered the custom of releasing a prisoner at

Passover time. In desperation he gave the crowd the choice between having Jesus Christ or Jesus Barabbas released. The crowd chose Jesus Barabbas and once again Pilate had to do something with Jesus; inaction was impossible.

We are no different from Pilate. Time after time we try to avoid making a decision about Jesus. Somehow we think that we can be neutral. But Jesus himself said, 'He who is not with me is against me.'[11] The choice before us is quite simple; we must either accept Jesus Christ as the Son of God and the Saviour of sinners or reject him. There is no middle way. To accept him means that we come to him confessing our sins, asking for his forgiveness, making him Lord of our lives.

Let us face Pilate's question: 'What shall I do with Jesus?' The decision that he faced is the same decision that faces us. Each of us must do something with Jesus. We can either follow the crowd and crucify him, or crown him Lord of our lives. What is your choice? The verdict is yours.

Notes

1. Matthew 27:22.
2. Acts 10:42.
3. John 8:58, 59.
4. John 14:30.
5. John 8:29.
6. John 5:18.
7. John 10:31–33.
8. Quoted by Vernon C. Grounds in *The Reason of our Hope* (Moody Press).

9. *Miracles* (Fontana).
10. *Mere Christianity* (Fontana).
11. Matthew 12:30.

Appendix:
The Records of the Case

The arrest—John 18:1–11

When he had finished praying, Jesus left with his disciples and crossed the Kidron Valley. On the other side there was an olive grove, and he and his disciples went into it.

Now Judas, who betrayed him, knew the place, because Jesus had often met there with his disciples. So Judas came to the grove, guiding a detachment of soldiers and some officials from the chief priests and Pharisees. They were carrying torches, lanterns and weapons.

Jesus, knowing all that was going to happen to him, went out and asked them, 'Who is it you want?'

'Jesus of Nazareth,' they replied.

'I am he,' Jesus said. (And Judas the traitor was standing there with them.) When Jesus said, 'I am he,' they drew back and fell to the ground.

Again he asked them, 'Who is it you want?'

And they said, 'Jesus of Nazareth.'

'I told you that I am he,' Jesus answered. 'If you are looking for me, then let these men go.' This happened so that the words he had spoken would be fulfilled: 'I have not lost one of those you gave me.'

Then Simon Peter, who had a sword, drew it and struck the high priest's servant, cutting off his right ear. (The servant's name was Malchus.)

Jesus commanded Peter, 'Put your sword away! Shall I not drink the cup the Father has given me?'

The Jewish trial
The examination before Annas—John 18:12–14 and 19–24

Then the detachment of soldiers with its commander and the Jewish officials arrested Jesus. They bound him and brought him first to Annas, who was the father-in-law of Caiaphas, the high priest that year. Caiaphas was the one who had advised the Jews that it would be good if one man died for the people.

Meanwhile, the high priest questioned Jesus about his disciples and his teaching.

'I have spoken openly to the world,' Jesus replied. 'I always taught in synagogues or at the temple, where all the Jews come together. I said nothing in secret. Why question me? Ask those who heard me. Surely they know what I said.'

When Jesus said this, one of the officials near by struck him in the face. 'Is that any way to answer the high priest?' he demanded.

'If I said something wrong,' Jesus replied, 'testify as to what is wrong. But if I spoke the truth, why did you strike me?' Then Annas sent him, still bound, to Caiaphas the high priest.

The first trial before Caiaphas and the Sanhedrin — Mark 14:53–65

They took Jesus to the high priest, and all the chief priests, elders and teachers of the law came together. Peter followed him at a distance, right into the court-yard of the high priest. There he sat with the guards and warmed himself at the fire.

The chief priests and the whole Sanhedrin were looking for evidence against Jesus so that they could put him to death, but they did not find any. Many testified falsely against him, but their statements did not agree.

Then some stood up and gave this false testimony against him: 'We heard him say, "I will destroy this man-made temple and in three days will build another, not made by man." ' Yet even then their testimony did not agree.

Then the high priest stood up before them and asked Jesus, 'Are you not going to answer? What is this testimony that these men are bringing against you?' But Jesus remained silent and gave no answer.

Again the high priest asked him, 'Are you the Christ, the Son of the Blessed One?'

'I am,' said Jesus. 'And you will see the Son of Man sitting at the right hand of the Mighty One and coming on the clouds of heaven.'

The high priest tore his clothes. 'Why do we need any more witnesses?' he asked. 'You have heard the blasphemy. What do you think?'

They all condemned him as worthy of death. Then some began to spit at him; they blindfolded him, struck him with their fists, and said, 'Prophesy!' And the guards took him and beat him.

Second trial before the Sanhedrin—Luke 22:66–71

At daybreak the council of the elders of the people, both the chief priests and teachers of the law, met together, and Jesus was led before them. 'If you are the Christ,' they said, 'tell us.'

Jesus answered, 'If I tell you, you will not believe me, and if I asked you, you would not answer. But from now on, the Son of Man will be seated at the right hand of the mighty God.'

They all asked, 'Are you then the Son of God?'

He replied, 'You are right in saying I am.'

Then they said, 'Why do we need any more testimony? We have heard it from his own lips.'

The first Roman trial

The indictment—John 18:28–31
Then the Jews led Jesus from Caiaphas to the palace of the Roman governor. By now it was early morning, and to avoid ceremonial uncleanness the Jews did not enter the palace; they wanted to be able to eat the Passover. So Pilate came out to them and asked, 'What charges are you bringing against this man?'

'If he were not a criminal,' they replied, 'we would not have handed him over to you.'

Pilate said, 'Take him yourselves and judge him by your own law.'

'But we have no right to execute anyone,' the Jews objected.

The examination — John 18:33–35
Pilate then went back inside the palace, summoned Jesus and asked him, 'Are you the king of the Jews?'

'Is that your own idea,' Jesus asked, 'or did others talk to you about me?'

'Do you think I am a Jew?' Pilate replied, 'It was your people and your chief priests who handed you over to me. What is it you have done?'

The defence — John 18:36–38
Jesus said, 'My kingdom is not of this world. If it were, my servants would fight to prevent my arrest by the Jews. But now my kingdom is from another place.'

'You are a king, then!' said Pilate.

Jesus answered, 'You are right in saying I am a king. In fact, for this reason I was born, and for this I came into the world, to testify to the truth. Everyone on the side of truth listens to me.'

'What is truth?' Pilate asked.

The acquittal — John 18:38
With this he went out again to the Jews and said, 'I find no basis for a charge against him.'

Trial before Herod — Luke 23:5–12

But they insisted, 'He stirs up the people all over Judea by his teaching. He started in Galilee and has come all the way here.'

On hearing this, Pilate asked if the man was a Galilean. When he learned that Jesus was under Herod's jurisdiction, he sent him to Herod, who was also in Jerusalem at that time.

When Herod saw Jesus, he was greatly pleased, because for a long time he had been wanting to see him. From what he had heard about him, he hoped to see him perform some miracle. He plied him with many questions, but Jesus gave him no answer. The chief priests and the teachers of the law were standing there, vehemently accusing him. Then Herod and his soldiers ridiculed and mocked him. Dressing him in an elegant robe, they sent him back to Pilate. That day Herod and Pilate became friends—before this they had been enemies.

The second Roman trial

Acquittal confirmed—Luke 23:13–16
Pilate called together the chief priests, the rulers and the people, and said to them, 'You brought me this man as one who was inciting the people to rebellion. I have examined him in your presence and have found no basis for your charges against him. Neither has Herod, for he sent him back to us; as you can see, he has done nothing to deserve death. Therefore, I will punish him and then release him.'

Barabbas—Pilate's wife—Matthew 27:15–23
Now it was the governor's custom at the Feast to release a prisoner chosen by the crowd. At that time they had a notorious prisoner, called Barabbas. So when the crowd had gathered, Pilate asked them, 'Which one do you want me to release to you: Barabbas, or Jesus who is called Christ?' For he knew it was out of envy that they had handed Jesus over to him.

While Pilate was sitting on the judge's seat, his wife sent him this message: 'Don't have anything to do with that innocent man, for I have suffered a great deal today in a dream because of him.'

But the chief priests and the elders persuaded the crowd to ask for Barabbas and to have Jesus executed.

'Which of the two do you want me to release to you?' asked the governor.

'Barabbas,' they answered.

'What shall I do, then, with Jesus who is called Christ?' Pilate asked.

They all answered, 'Crucify him!'

'Why? What crime has he committed?' asked Pilate.

But they shouted all the louder, 'Crucify him!'

Final hearing and sentence — John 19:1–16
Then Pilate took Jesus and had him flogged. The soldiers twisted together a crown of thorns and put it on his head. They clothed him in a purple robe and went up to him again and again, saying, 'Hail, O king of the Jews!' And they struck him in the face.

Once more Pilate came out and said to the Jews, 'Look, I am bringing him out to you to let you know that I find no basis for a charge against him.' When Jesus came out wearing the crown of thorns and the purple robe, Pilate said to them, 'Here is the man!'

As soon as the chief priests and their officials saw him, they shouted, 'Crucify! Crucify!'

But Pilate answered, 'You take him and crucify him. As for me, I find no basis for a charge against him.'

The Jews insisted, 'We have a law, and according to that law he must die, because he claimed to be the Son of God.'

When Pilate heard this, he was even more afraid, and he went back inside the palace. 'Where do you come from?' he asked Jesus, but Jesus gave him no answer. 'Do you refuse to speak to me?' Pilate said. 'Don't you realise I have power either to free you or to crucify you?'

Jesus answered, 'You would have no power over me if it were not given to you from above. Therefore the one who handed me over to you is guilty of a greater sin.'

From then on, Pilate tried to set Jesus free, but the Jews kept shouting, 'If you let this man go, you are no friend of Caesar. Anyone who claims to be a king opposes Caesar.'

When Pilate heard this, he brought Jesus out and sat down on the judge's seat at a place known as The Stone Pavement (which in Aramaic is Gabbatha). It was the day of Preparation of Passover Week, about the sixth hour.

'Here is your king,' Pilate said to the Jews.

But they shouted, 'Take him away! Take him away! Crucify him!'

'Shall I crucify your king?' Pilate asked.

'We have no king but Caesar,' the chief priests answered.

Finally Pilate handed him over to them to be crucified.